A Creative Approach t
Teaching Science

Nicky Waller

B L O O M S B U R Y
LONDON · OXFORD · NEW YORK · NEW DELHI · SYDNEY

Bloomsbury Education

An imprint of Bloomsbury Publishing Plc

50 Bedford Square	1385 Broadway
London	New York
WC1B 3DP	NY 10018
UK	USA

www.bloomsbury.com

BLOOMSBURY and the Diana logo are trademarks of Bloomsbury Publishing Plc

First published in Great Britain 2017

© Nicky Waller, 2017

Illustrations © Tamara Joubert, 2017

British Library Cataloguing-in-Publication Data
A catalogue record for this book is available from the British Library.

Library of Congress Cataloguing-in-Publication data has been applied for.
ISBN:
PB: 978-1-4729-4172-5
ePub: 978-1-4729-4171-8
ePDF: 978-1-4729-4173-2

2 4 6 8 10 9 7 5 3 1

Typeset by Newgen Knowledge Works (P) ltd., Chennai, India
Printed and bound in the UK by CPI Group Ltd, Croydon, CR0 4YY

To find out more about our authors and books visit www.bloomsbury.com. Here you will find extracts, author
interviews, details of forthcoming events and the option to sign up for our newsletters.

To Mum and Dad . . .
for never doubting

Contents

Introduction   1

Biology   3

1 Plants   5
Year 1   5
Year 2   9
Year 3   11

2 Animals including Humans   17
Year 1   17
Year 2   23
Year 3   28
Year 4   32
Year 5   36
Year 6   37

3 Living Things and their Habitats   43
Year 2   43
Year 4   48
Year 5   51
Year 6   55

4 Seasonal Changes   59
Year 1   59

5 Evolution and Inheritance   67
Year 6   67

Chemistry   73

6 Materials   75
Year 1   75
Year 2   80

Materials (continued)

Year 3		84
Year 4		84
Year 5		91

7 Rocks — 99

Year 3 — 99

Physics — 105

8 Light — 107

Year 3 — 107
Year 6 — 112

9 Sound — 117

Year 4 — 117

10 Forces and Magnets — 123

Year 3 — 123
Year 5 — 128

11 Electricity — 135

Year 4 — 135
Year 6 — 141

12 Earth and Space — 145

Year 5 — 145

Index — 152

Introduction

Since the introduction of the new National Curriculum in England, published November 2013 and made statutory for most year groups from September 2014, many primary school teachers confess to delivering the bare minimum of the Programmes of Study for science, describing how there just isn't enough time to devote their attention to the 'poor man's core subject'. With many new statutory requirements to teach and attain mastery of and the ever-increasing pressure to reach expected standards in English and mathematics, it is often an enticing, time-saving option to download a basic plan from a free online site, with little regard to innovation or creativity.

There is great potential for primary teachers to feel uninspired whilst planning and delivering what could easily be interpreted as quite low-level thinking tasks. Many of the statutory requirements for science refer to pupils being able to identify, name, label, group and describe the world around them, rather than, as is stated in the Purpose of Study for science, develop a sense of excitement and curiosity about natural phenomena.

But all is not lost. More recently there has been a ripple of excitement within the world of primary science as science leaders and teachers have felt the impetus to raise the profile of this subject once again and search for alternative ways to breathe life back into the science curriculum. Some schools have made a huge investment into purchasing published schemes of work for science whilst others continue to spend hours searching the internet for inspirational ideas. In this book I am hoping to demonstrate that you can cover the full curriculum without your teaching being dry and uninspired.

Bringing creativity back to science

This book has been written to help bring creativity back to primary science. It contains a wealth of exciting and unusual activities that have been tried and tested, evaluated and improved over more than 20 years of teaching experience. It is intended to be used as a 'one stop shop' for busy primary teachers, crammed full of ideas for how to ensure progression of the statutory requirements for primary science, from Year 1 to Year 6, in an innovative and memorable way.

Creativity in science can be many things, from an unusual starting point which serves to motivate and challenge children as they embark on a new activity, to an innovative strategy of recording and presenting, to an inspired way of linking different areas of the curriculum which enables science learning to become more meaningful and deeply embedded. Well thought out primary science lessons should not be about children producing pages and pages of formal experimental write-up but rather about them thinking, discussing, trying things out, getting their hands dirty, working inside and outdoors and, of course, having fun whilst learning!

When some form of recording in science is required, this should be focused to allow for high quality formative assessment enabling children to make progress in that specific area or skill. Focused recording can be extremely creative, for example children could sort and group real items made from a variety of materials using a gigantic sorting circle created in the school hall (rather than sticking printed pictures onto a pre-drawn Venn diagram) or they could identify patterns in data by sketching a line graph on the playground using chalk (rather than agonising over axes and scales on graph paper).

The skills of enquiry should be at the heart of every science activity and this no longer means children merely carrying out a fair test investigation at the end of every topic. Children should be encouraged to work scientifically by questioning, observing, measuring, planning, researching, recording, presenting and evaluating at every opportunity. This book contains suggestions for which skills might be best suited to each of the activities or strategies described and these can be found under the 'Working Scientifically' headings accompanying each activity. The aim is for enquiry to form a common thread, helping children to understand that science is just as much about what they do as about what they know.

One final note is that the creative strategies and ideas contained in this book have been grouped into the topic areas of biology, chemistry and physics and presented with reference to the relevant age groups, as recommended in the National Curriculum for England. However, it must be remembered that the topics described for each year group are only suggested and teachers should bear in mind that schools are only required to teach the relevant programmes of study by the end of the key stage. Beginning to feel inspired? Go on... be creative!

Biology

1
Plants

Learning about plants affords many practical opportunities to link with other biology topics such as 'Seasonal Changes' in Year 1 and 'Living Things and their Habitats' in Years 2, 4, 5 and 6. Children should be encouraged to work outside in the school and local environment as much as possible in order to observe where, when and how varieties of plants grow and change throughout the year.

Plants in Year 1

> **Statutory Requirement:** identify and name a variety of common wild and garden plants, including deciduous and evergreen trees.

To build familiarity and confidence with naming plants, children should get out and about either in the school grounds or on a planned visit to a local park at different times of the year. A simple 'I-spy' sheet can be created prior to the adventure which includes labelled photographs of plants the children are very likely to see.

Children could also take their own photographs of the plants they identify and these could be printed, named and fastened together with a treasury tag or split pin to make a swatch book. Give the activity a real purpose by loaning the completed guide to another class to use on their 'I-spy' trail and then asking them for feedback on the usefulness of this secondary source.

Working scientifically
- **Observing closely, using simple equipment**
- **Identifying and classifying**
- **Gathering and recording data to help in answering questions**

Flower power

A seasonal spotter trail in the spring time is a great way for children to learn the names of flowering plants as they begin to appear with the warmer weather and then again in the summer when many more flowers are in full bloom (see 'Seasonal Changes' activities described on page 59).

Flowers can be identified and then preserved by placing fresh, dry flowers face down in between the centre pages of a thick, heavy book for at least two weeks. Flowers such as roses, daisies and pansies work particularly well. Children will also have great fun using flower petals to make perfumes and potions!

Challenge children to try some flower-related tasks such as: Who can make the longest daisy chain? or Who can grow the tallest sunflower? They could explore flower-related myths and questions such as:

- Can we really tell the time by blowing the seeds from a dandelion head?
- Can you tell if someone likes butter by holding a buttercup under their chin?
- Are snowdrops really made of snow?
- Why do we wear poppies on Remembrance Sunday?

Finally, there are lots of creative role play opportunities for Year 1 children to practise and apply their new found knowledge of flowering plants. Perhaps they could be florists, sending and receiving orders for a range of common wild and garden flowers. A selection of real and artificial plants could be used for identification and arrangement.

Working scientifically

- **Asking simple questions and recognising that they can be answered in different ways**
- **Observing closely, using simple equipment**
- **Identifying and classifying**
- **Using their observations and ideas to suggest answers to questions**
- **Gathering and recording data to help in answering questions**

Articulate through art

There are some fantastic art projects that can be used when identifying and naming common plants, in particular flowering plants. Spring celebrations such as Mother's Day and Easter provide perfect opportunities for children to engage in observational drawing, junk modelling, collage, painting and printing to allow them to create representations of the flowers they are able to identify and name.

Working scientifically

- **Observing closely, using simple equipment**
- **Identifying and classifying**
- **Gathering and recording data to help in answering questions**

Identifying fruits and vegetables

Young children may not consider the fruits and vegetables they eat and see in the shops or markets to be plants. However, a visit to a local allotment, vegetable patch or raised beds will help them to understand that these can be grown relatively simply from seeds. Some of the easiest fruits and vegetables to grow with children are sugar snap peas, cabbages, potatoes, strawberries and cherry tomatoes. Particularly fast growing vegetable plants include mustard seeds, cress, radishes, broad beans and chives.

Learning the names of a range of common fruit and vegetable plants can lead to a range of other activities such as sorting and grouping, tasting, cooking, data handling with pictograms, simple bar charts and tally charts as well as printing and painting.

Working scientifically

- **Observing closely, using simple equipment**
- **Identifying and classifying**
- **Using their observations and ideas to suggest answers to questions**
- **Gathering and recording data to help in answering questions**

Labelling leaves

Children will enjoy collecting as many interesting leaves as they can in a paper bag and then using simple pre-made spotter sheets to identify and name them. They could record their findings by creating a leaf person or animal and then labelling the leaves by writing or sticking the name next to each one for identification. An enchanting book, *Leaf Man* by Lois Ehlert makes a perfect accompaniment to this activity.

Identifying trees

Young children often fail to realise that a tree is a giant plant which grows from a seed. Tree identification in Year 1 works well by giving children a number of named leaves and asking them to 'find a tree that has leaves like this'. The investigation 'Evergreen and deciduous' described in the 'Seasonal Changes' topic (on page 59) will help children begin to understand why some trees lose their leaves in the autumn and should be accompanied by them wrapping up warm and heading outside to identify a range of deciduous and evergreen trees.

Working scientifically

- **Observing closely, using simple equipment**
- **Identifying and classifying**
- **Gathering and recording data to help in answering questions**

> **Statutory Requirement:** identify and describe the basic structure of a variety of common flowering plants, including trees.

Parts of a plant

The best way for children to learn about the structure of flowering plants is to handle them, take them apart, look at each part closely using a hand lens and piece them back together again! Remember to include potted plants or those growing outside so that children can feel the tugging of roots as they are pulled out of the soil. Separating the flower, stem, leaves and roots will help children to identify and name these parts. However, it is not until Year 3 that children are required to identify and describe the functions of different parts of flowering plants (as described on page 13).

Don't forget to examine and label trees too. Children could lay long pieces of string or rope along the ground to predict how far-reaching the hidden roots might be. They will be amazed to learn that the roots should spread at least as far out as the tree is tall!

Working scientifically

- **Observing closely, using simple equipment**
- **Identifying and classifying**

Articulate through art

A motivating way for young children to record the different parts of a common flowering plant is for them to create and label a collage using materials such as cake cases, art straws, green tissue paper and brown wool. A simple 3D model looks really effective placed on a shelf with brown wool hanging down from the underside of the shelf to represent the roots growing below the surface. Children in Year 1 could share their collage or models with children in Year 3 or Year 5 who should be able to label the parts of the flower in more detail as they learn about the life cycle of a flowering plant (see page 15) and plant reproduction (see page 53).

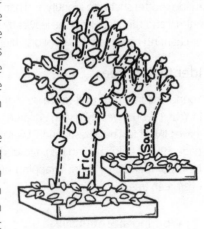

Children could create a 'forest of trees' by drawing the outline from their elbow, along their forearm (trunk), around their hand span (branches) and back down to the elbow again onto strong, thick card. Once cut out and decorated with seasonal leaves, they can be displayed in an upright position and labelled to show children's understanding of the basic structure of a tree.

Working scientifically

- **Identifying and classifying**
- **Gathering and recording data to help in answering questions**

Which part can we eat?

It is important for children to understand that many types of plants can be used as food and that we can eat different parts of some plants. Use a selection of vegetables for children to attempt to identify, name and suggest which part of the plant each one comes from, such as:

- spinach, cabbage and lettuce are the leaves
- carrot, turnip and radish are the roots
- celery and rhubarb are the stem
- broccoli and cauliflower are the flower
- corn or peas are the seeds of a plant.

Working scientifically
- **Asking simple questions and recognising that they can be answered in different ways**
- **Identifying and classifying**
- **Using their observations and ideas to suggest answers to questions**

Plants in Year 2

Statutory Requirement: observe and describe how seeds and bulbs grow into mature plants.

This objective enables children to make careful observations over time. Photographs could be taken at every stage of a bulb or seed's development and then sequenced correctly using a scrap book, photo album, diary/journal (in the shape of a seed or bulb), flip book, zigzag book, PowerPoint presentation or time-lapse video. There are also superb links to the mathematics curriculum whereby children compare and measure lengths and heights and then record these using simple charts and graphs.

Observing plants from bulbs

Explain to children that some plants grow from bulbs and that true bulbs, such as tulips, onions and daffodils, contain a complete miniature plant inside with leaves, stem and even flower buds! Cutting them in half and examining using a hand lens is always a fascinating activity.

Children could plant bulbs (pointy tip facing up) in a clear container about three quarters filled with stones or pebbles so that they can observe both the roots and shoots growing. They should add water until it is just covering the bottom of the bulb and keep replacing this as the level decreases over time. Children should place their container on a sunny window spot next to a long vertical strip of card so that they can mark and date the growth of the shoots (and roots) every two to three days until the bulb blossoms. The whole class could plant spring bulbs such as daffodils, hyacinths and tulips either directly in the ground or in a container – this should be done at the start of the school year in September and October.

Observing plants from seeds

Children should understand that most plants grow from seeds and that these come in many different shapes, sizes and types. Fast growing seeds such as mustard and cress can easily be grown in a week to ten days on a damp piece of kitchen roll, cotton wool or a small amount of compost in a shallow tray, ensuring that the growing medium never dries out. A creative approach to this activity is for children to scatter seeds in the shape of their hand print, the first letter of their name or within the boundaries of interesting cookie cutters such as stars or love hearts and then observe them growing in fascinating shapes.

Growing a bean seed such as a broad or runner bean can be done by rolling damp sheets of kitchen roll or blotting paper into a tube, inserting this into a clear glass jar and then wedging the bean seed between the damp paper and the side of the jar. Add some water to the bottom of the jar and keep this topped up. Children can observe both the roots and shoots growing and record observations and/or measurements of this over time. They could eventually transfer their bean into a small pot of compost and take it home to enjoy its continued growth.

If possible, children could take ownership of a raised bed, greenhouse or patch of land in or nearby to school. Alternatively they could use unusual containers for planting such as plastic bottles, old wellington boots, teapots and watering cans (remember to drill holes in the bottom so the water can drain out easily). Quick growing flowers that can be planted from seeds throughout the year include sweet peas, nasturtiums, marigolds, poppies, sunflowers and mixed wild flowers. Ask children which seeds they would like to plant and devise a schedule of operation.

Grow a 'grass hair' family

A fun way to capture young children's interest and imagination when planting and growing seeds is to grow a grass character and make careful observations and measurements of its sprouting 'hair' over a period of two weeks. Children should drop a handful of fast-growing grass seeds into the foot of a pop sock, add at least three large handfuls of compost, twist the sock until it is the size and shape of a tennis ball and tie a knot. They can personalise their 'family member' by sticking on googly eyes and a mouth.

Next, children should wet the 'head' by dunking it in a bowl of cold water and then place it on a clean yoghurt pot half-filled with water (so that the stocking tail dangles into the water). Grass will grow in a sunny window spot but ensure the pot is refilled with water every few days.

An alternative way to achieve this is to fill a clear plastic cup almost to the top with compost, sprinkle on some fast-growing grass seeds and keep these moist by spraying them with water every few days. Children can personalise the cup with a printed photograph of their own face.

Working scientifically

- **Observing closely, using simple equipment**
- **Gathering and recording data to help in answering questions**

> **Statutory Requirement:** find out and describe how plants need water, light and a suitable temperature to grow and stay healthy.

Begin this activity with four 'grass hair' characters (see activity above) that you have been growing for two weeks at home and ask the children for their help saying you can't understand what has happened to their 'hair': one remains lush and green (grown in a sunny spot), one has turned yellow (grown in the dark) and two others have gone brown and withered (one was given no water after one week and another was grown in the fridge). Can the children suggest what might be the cause of these unusual changes?

This scenario could lead to children investigating simple conditions required for healthy plant growth. They could set up their own trials, using the grass they have grown, to find out what happens when some plants have had either water, light or warmth removed. This activity provides a basic introduction to the simple comparative and fair tests that children will become more confident with in lower Key Stage 2 (see activity on page 11 for advice on progression from Year 2 to Year 3 'requirements for life' plants investigation).

Working scientifically

- **Asking simple questions and recognising that they can be answered in different ways**
- **Observing closely, using simple equipment**
- **Performing simple tests**
- **Using their observations and ideas to suggest answers to questions**
- **Gathering and recording data to help in answering questions**

Plants in Year 3

> **Statutory Requirement:** explore the requirements of plants for life and growth (air, light, water, nutrients from soil, and room to grow) and how they vary from plant to plant.

The 'Grow a 'grass hair' family' activity on page 10 leads to Year 2 children investigating what happens to plants that have already begun to grow in a healthy environment before a basic requirement is removed (water, light or warmth). To make their investigations significantly different, Year 3 children could find out if plants will grow from seeds with a wider range of independent variables to explore.

Note: Mustard or cress seeds work well and are fast growing, however, any seeds can be used for investigation, e.g. children could compare broccoli seeds, lettuce seeds and pea seeds to find out how growth might vary from plant to plant.

Ask groups of children to make a list of what plants need in order to grow. They should discuss their ideas before selecting one of these variables to investigate further and find out what happens when this (and only this) is removed. Don't forget to include a 'control' specimen for comparison whereby the same number of seeds are planted and grown with all of the necessary requirements for life. Groups could consider:

Air – Will seeds grow without air? How can I remove the air but ensure the seeds still get light? How can I remove the air but still water my seeds when required?

Light – Will seeds grow without light? Where can I put them to ensure there is no light? How can I water them without exposing them to light?

Water – Will seeds grow without water? Where can I ensure they will remain dry? Will seeds grow using different liquids other than water?

Nutrients from soil – Will seeds grow without soil? Will seeds grow in other materials? What other materials can I use? Will seeds grow faster or healthier in soil that has added nutrients? How can I add nutrients to soil?

Room to grow – Will seeds grow if I plant them far apart from each other or very close together or on top of each other?

Children take great pleasure in investigating an enquiry question they have devised for themselves as they take ownership of the investigation and feel motivated to find answers. Their observations, comparisons and measurements could be recorded creatively using charts, graphs, timelines, diaries, photographs and video.

Working scientifically

- **Asking relevant questions and using different types of scientific enquiries to answer them**
- **Setting up simple practical enquiries, comparative and fair tests**
- **Making systematic and careful observations and, where appropriate, taking accurate measurements using standard units, using a range of equipment**
- **Gathering, recording, classifying and presenting data in a variety of ways to help in answering questions**
- **Recording findings using simple scientific language, drawings, labelled diagrams, keys, bar charts and tables**
- **Reporting on findings from enquiries, including oral and written explanations, displays or presentations of results and conclusions**
- **Using results to draw simple conclusions, make predictions for new values, suggest improvements and raise further questions**
- **Identifying differences, similarities or changes related to simple scientific ideas and processes**
- **Using straightforward scientific evidence to answer questions or to support their findings**

> **Statutory Requirement:** identify and describe the functions of different parts of flowering plants: roots, stem/trunk, leaves and flowers.

This objective follows on from work in the Year 1 Plants topic described on page 8 whereby children learn to identify and describe the basic structure of a variety of common flowering plants. To develop higher order thinking, children could consider what would happen to a plant if it did not have: flowers; a stem; leaves; roots and then explain why this would happen. This question also offers a creative approach to pre and post topic assessment.

Ouch! (1)

As in Year 1, children should identify the parts of a range of flowering plants using a hands-on approach. The roots, stem, leaves and flowers of small flowering plants could be placed carefully next to their corresponding label onto pre-cut strips of sticky back plastic which is then folded over to secure them in place and create a bookmark as a simple reminder of plant parts and their names.

Working scientifically

- **Gathering, recording, classifying and presenting data in a variety of ways to help in answering questions**

Ouch! (2)

To learn about what specific plant parts do, children could remove either the leaves or roots from a number of healthy plants growing in soil and observe what happens to them over a number of weeks, with sunlight and regular watering, compared to plants that have not had leaves or roots removed.

There are opportunities for creative recording here whereby children take comparison photographs each day over a period of up to four weeks. The photographs could be uploaded to a PowerPoint presentation and set to a brief slide transition time or linked together as a time-lapse recording documenting change over time.

Working scientifically

- **Setting up simple practical enquiries, comparative and fair tests**
- **Making systematic and careful observations and, where appropriate, taking accurate measurements using standard units, using a range of equipment**
- **Gathering, recording, classifying and presenting data in a variety of ways to help in answering questions**
- **Recording findings using simple scientific language, drawings, labelled diagrams, keys, bar charts and tables**
- **Reporting on findings from enquiries, including oral and written explanations, displays or presentations of results and conclusions**
- **Using results to draw simple conclusions, make predictions for new values, suggest improvements and raise further questions**
- **Identifying differences, similarities or changes related to simple scientific ideas and processes**

The answer is blowing in the wind

When learning about the function of the roots in anchoring a plant, children should have opportunities to feel the resisting force exerted as a plant is being uprooted. They could wait for a particularly windy day or simulate this in the classroom using a powerful fan, to investigate what happens to a plant that has had its roots removed and placed back into the soil (plants with tall stems work well for this).

> Working scientifically
> - **Setting up simple practical enquiries, comparative and fair tests**
> - **Making systematic and careful observations**
> - **Reporting on findings from enquiries, including oral and written explanations, displays or presentations of results and conclusions**

> **Statutory Requirement:** investigate the way in which water is transported within plants.

How do plants get water? (1)

Children will enjoy learning about the functions of the stem of a plant by revisiting and extending a popular activity they may remember from their days in Nursery or Reception. Placing white flowers such as roses or carnations in coloured water (use plenty of good quality food colouring) is a great way for children to observe the leaves and flowers change colour as water is transported up the stem. You could also model this process by placing one end of a strip of white kitchen roll into coloured water and observing how the water travels up the paper. This activity also works well using fresh leafy stalks of celery. For further exploration, children should cut the celery open to see exactly where the coloured water has transported up the stem.

How do plants get water? (2)

Choose a tree and attach an empty clear plastic bag to a branch by enclosing the leaves and sealing the bag (or tying the handles in a knot) to keep it in place. After a week, children will observe that the bag looks misty and now contains water. Can they suggest where the water has come from and why this has appeared? Recap that plants, including trees, absorb nutrients and water from the soil through their roots. The water flows through the trunk (stem) of the tree, along the branches and to every leaf. The leaves use the water, with other things like sunlight and carbon dioxide, to make their food and stay healthy. Some of this water is returned to the air and this is what they have captured in their bag.

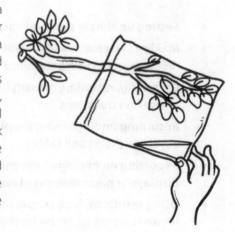

Working scientifically

- **Setting up simple practical enquiries, comparative and fair tests**
- **Making systematic and careful observations**
- **Reporting on findings from enquiries, including oral and written explanations, displays or presentations of results and conclusions**
- **Using results to draw simple conclusions, make predictions for new values, suggest improvements and raise further questions**
- **Identifying differences, similarities or changes related to simple scientific ideas and processes**
- **Using straightforward scientific evidence to answer questions or to support their findings**

> **Statutory Requirement:** explore the part that flowers play in the life cycle of flowering plants, including pollination, seed formation and seed dispersal.

Children should understand that flowers are often brightly coloured and scented to attract insects and birds to begin the process of pollination. The whole class could carry out a colour survey of flowering plants in the school grounds, local environment or their own gardens. They could predict which colour petals might be the most and least frequent and make suggestions for why this might be.

Working scientifically

- **Making systematic and careful observations**
- **Recording findings using simple scientific language, drawings, labelled diagrams, keys, bar charts and tables**
- **Using straightforward scientific evidence to answer questions or to support their findings**

Learning through role play

Children should have opportunities to examine the inner workings of a real flowering plant, such as a daffodil or lily, in order to identify the parts crucial to reproduction. Explain that the dark coloured pollen stored on the anthers of the male part often rubs onto the wings or body of insects as they feed on sweet nectar found at the base of the flower. To model this, use a cheesy flavoured puff crisp to represent the anther covered in pollen. Ask children to feel this between their fingers and thumbs and then observe how the orange flavouring rubs off easily onto their skin.

Children should also look closely or feel how the female part, called the stigma, is sticky in order to 'catch' the pollen grains when the insect visits another flower – this process of transferring pollen from the anthers of one flower to the stigma of another flower is called pollination.

Ask two volunteers to represent flowering plants such as the ones they have examined in detail. Each child should stretch their arms out and wear a pair of gloves to represent the anthers of the plant. Place tiny pompoms onto their palms facing up to represent the pollen grains they have produced and are storing here. Each 'flower' should also wear a hat or cap to represent the stigma and this can be made sticky by carefully placing a small amount of clear hair gel on top.

Ask one final volunteer to represent an insect in search of nectar (they could wear wings if they wish to). As they do so, they should collect a small number of pollen grains (pompoms) from one flower and drop them so that some land on the sticky stigma (hat) of another flower.

The pollinated 'flower' can then collect their pompom 'pollen' and hold this in clenched fists around the height of their chin to represent how the pollen has travelled to the ovary of the plant, where new seeds are made. They will need to exchange the pompoms for real seeds (sunflower seeds work well in this model as they are a good size) to model the process of seed formation. Children should have opportunities to identify the ovary of a real flower at this stage too and they might wish to look inside for seeds that have been produced.

The 'flower' should now scatter the seeds as far away as possible by throwing them in different directions so that they will have a greater chance of growing into new plants. This represents the process of seed dispersal. Photographs could be taken at each stage of the role play activity, ordered chronologically and accompanied with an appropriate descriptive text.

Working scientifically

- **Gathering, recording, classifying and presenting data in a variety of ways to help in answering questions**

2
A Creative Approach to Teaching Animals including Humans

'Animals including Humans' is the only science topic to appear in every year group throughout the primary age range. Children will progress from naming body parts in Year 1 to knowing about bones and muscles in Year 3 to describing the digestive system in Year 4 and the circulatory system in Year 6. They will also learn about animal groups, what animals eat and their life cycles.

Animals including Humans in Year 1

Quite often, Year 1 teachers divide the statutory requirements for this topic into two separate units in which children will learn about animals. They might begin by exploring a range of animals kept as pets, found at the farm or zoo and in different countries before learning about what it means to be a human. This concept alone might pose problems for our youngest scientists who often fail to believe that a human could ever be an animal!

> **Statutory Requirement:** identify and name a variety of common animals including fish, amphibians, reptiles, birds and mammals.

Visits out and visitors in

The most obvious way to ensure that children are familiar with and confident naming a variety of common animals is to visit to a local farm or zoo in order to see and handle the animals first-hand. Alternatively, you could arrange for a visit from a company specialising in bringing animals into school.

Bring your (toy) animal to school

Children will delight in bringing their very own toy animal in from home when requested at the start of this topic. Encourage them to bring a wide variety of fluffy/cuddly/plastic/model animals and be prepared to include some additional ones to ensure an interesting and varied selection. Individuals should talk about the animal they have brought in before engaging in some simple, whole class classifying and grouping activities. They could place their animal in the appropriate sorting hoop when asked questions such as:

- Can you keep your animal as a pet?
- Can your animal fly?
- Does your animal live in water?
- Does your animal lay eggs?
- Does your animal have feathers?

Choose your questions carefully so that they lead children to begin thinking about what it means to be a mammal, reptile, amphibian, bird or fish and the simple characteristics that might be used to identify and classify them. Children should be encouraged to devise and ask their own questions and then 'be the judge' of how their classmates perform in the resulting sorting and grouping tasks.

Working scientifically
- **Asking simple questions and recognising that they can be answered in different ways**
- **Observing closely**
- **Identifying and classifying**
- **Using their observations and ideas to suggest answers to questions**
- **Gathering and recording data to help in answering questions**

Animals in books

Animal themed story books are a creative secondary source of information. Classic titles such as *Rumble in the Jungle*, *Commotion in the Ocean* or *Cock-a Doodle-do!* by Giles Andreae, *What the Ladybird Heard* by Julia Donaldson and *Big Red Bath* by Julia Jarman and Adrian Reynolds are all great examples to get children thinking, identifying and naming common animals.

Two particular favourites of mine are the books: *Creaturepedia* by Adrienne Brown, which is a collection of animals from all over the world, and *Just Imagine* by Nick Sharratt and Pippa Goodhart which contains 50 individual and beautifully illustrated animals ranging from a polar bear to a sloth to a stick insect. Teachers could use these images to assess which animals children can identify and name both pre and post topic.

Working scientifically
- **Identifying and classifying**
- **Using their observations and ideas to suggest answers to questions**

How big? How small?

A motivating activity, which links perfectly with the Year 1 requirements for measurement in the mathematics curriculum, is to create a giant ruler with a roll of plain wall paper secured vertically to a wall or door in the classroom and mark a scale in 10 cm gradients. Children can use this to measure themselves and stick pictures of the animals they can name and have researched onto the ruler to indicate how tall they are too.

Statutory Requirement: identify and name a variety of common animals that are carnivores, herbivores and omnivores.

What's for dinner?

A creative way for children to sort and group animals according to the food they eat is to have three paper plates: one with a picture of meat stuck onto it, one with a picture of leaves stuck onto it and one with both (you should also write carnivore, herbivore or omnivore on the bottom of the equivalent plate but don't show this yet). Children can either arrange the toys they have brought in from home, small world animals or animal picture cards around the plates to show what they think each animal would eat. Take photographs of this for evidence before turning the plates over to reveal the new, key vocabulary of carnivore, herbivore and omnivore.

Identifying, classifying and sorting can also be done using animal shaped biscuits, crackers or crisps. The context of 'what animals eat' provides a perfect opportunity to introduce or reinforce the concept of overlapping hoops in a Venn diagram and creating an intersection for omnivores eating both meat and plants.

Open wide!

Children will enjoy making models or masks of different animals with a flap to lift and reveal inside the animals' mouths and the types of teeth they have. A crocodile or shark mask would have lots of sharp triangle shaped pointy teeth for ripping through meat, a cow or horse would have square and rectangle shaped flat teeth for chewing grass whereas a pig or bear would have both types of teeth. Children could research and compare a range of common animals' teeth and use this to determine whether they are carnivore, herbivore or omnivore.

Who is coming to tea?

There are obvious links with the classic children's book *The Tiger Who Came to Tea* by Judith Kerr as children consider the practicalities of the story in real-life! A list of food eaten by the tiger in the story includes sandwiches, buns, biscuits, cake, supper from the saucepans, food from the fridge as well as packets and tins from the cupboards. The tiger also had milk, tea, orange juice, beer and water to drink!

Children could compose their own, scientifically correct, versions of the story by choosing an animal and thinking about all the things that it would eat if it really was coming to tea. Linking science with the English curriculum, children could compile a class anthology of tales about carnivores, herbivores and omnivores to share with others.

Working scientifically

- **Identifying and classifying**
- **Using their observations and ideas to suggest answers to questions**
- **Gathering and recording data to help in answering questions**

> **Statutory Requirement:** describe and compare the structure of a variety of common animals (fish, amphibians, reptiles, birds and mammals, including pets).

Sort it out!

Ask children to sort the toys they have brought in from home according to the structure of their animal such as: Does your animal have legs? How many legs? Does your animal have a beak; tail; wings; mane; toes; ears; horns; fins? Again, children should be encouraged to devise and ask their own questions and then 'be the judge' of how their classmates perform in the resulting sorting and grouping tasks.

Working scientifically

- **Asking simple questions and recognising that they can be answered in different ways**
- **Identifying and classifying**
- **Using their observations and ideas to suggest answers to questions**
- **Gathering and recording data to help in answering questions**

Whose body part?

Show images of a range of animal parts such as a duck's webbed feet or an elephant's trunk and ask children to identify and name both the part and the animal. You could also make jigsaws by cutting out the heads, ears, bodies, tails and legs from pictures of common animals, mixing them all up in a bag and then inviting children to create either the original or an imaginary mixed-up animal.

A fun game to play is a variation on 'Heads, bodies and legs' whereby every child has a long strip of paper and is asked to think of an animal but keep this a secret. Children should draw only the head of their animal at the top of their paper and then fold this over so no-one can see what they have drawn before passing this to another child. The next step is to draw only the body of their chosen animal before passing the folded paper to a third child who will complete the animal by drawing its legs and feet and then pass the folded paper on one last time. Children will take great pleasure and amusement in revealing their animal hybrid and comparing the different structures.

> ## Working scientifically
> - **Identifying and classifying**
> - **Gathering and recording data to help in answering questions**

Animal x-rays

Examining x-rays is an interesting way for children to describe and compare the structure of a range of animals. A visit to school from a local vet would be an invaluable secondary source of information whereby children could plan and ask their own questions in order to extend their knowledge and understanding of animals and their bodies. Alternatively, animal x-ray resource packs and accompanying information can be purchased easily following a quick online search.

> ## Working scientifically
> - **Asking simple questions and recognising that they can be answered in different ways**
> - **Identifying and classifying**
> - **Ask people questions and use simple secondary sources to find answers (non-statutory notes and guidance)**

> **Statutory Requirement:** identify, name, draw and label the basic parts of the human body and say which part of the body is associated with each sense.

Explain to children that you have brought an animal toy in from home too and ask them to guess what it might be. You could give clues such as: this animal has two eyes, this animal has hair on its body, this animal is not born from an egg and this animal is a mammal. After a number of guesses, reveal a girl or boy doll and await children's responses. You could be met with laughter, disbelief, confusion or resistance so be prepared to argue your case!

Large scale labelling

Children choose a classmate to lie down on a rolled-out length of plain wallpaper and then draw around their outline. Small groups working together should locate, name and label (by writing on the wallpaper) as many different body parts as they can in an agreed amount of time. Having challenged Year 1 children to this task on many an occasion, I never cease to be amazed at the high level of response from some individuals!

A great way to extend the challenge is to give each group an envelope containing the names of parts they might not yet have identified, such as: shin, ankle, knee cap, thigh, waist, spine, shoulder, eye lid and nostril. Groups should share their ideas about where to place the additional labels as well as add even more of their own before counting up a total to compare with other groups.

Sing it, rhyme it, play it!

Singing popular songs with young children will help them to name, identify and remember different body parts.

Be sure to include:

- Heads, Shoulders, Knees and Toes
- One Finger, One Thumb Keep Moving
- Hokey Cokey
- If You're Happy and You Know It Clap Your Hands

Don't forget to play games such as 'Body parts bingo', 'Stick the sticky note on the body part' or 'Simon says' (whereby children have to put their hands on different body parts when instructed to by 'Simon'). These are superb ways of assessing which children are unsure of particular parts of the body – a common example of this is when young children confuse the elbows and shoulders, or the chin with shin!

Body part collage

Children can have great fun creating and labelling collages from different body parts they have cut out from newspapers, leaflets and magazines. They could be the fictional scientist Dr. Frankenstein designing a new monster human!

> **Working scientifically**
> - **Identifying and classifying**
> - **Using their observations and ideas to suggest answers to questions**
> - **Gathering and recording data to help in answering questions**

Investigating the five senses

Children working at the expected standard for this objective should be able to say which part of the body is associated with each sense. Simply recalling this information as fact requires quite low level thinking from children, therefore, opportunities to work scientifically and investigate the senses should be promoted wherever possible. Suggestions for enquiry activities could include:

- Seeing: use and explore with magnifying glasses, binoculars, microscopes, telescopes, periscopes, kaleidoscopes and torches.
- Hearing: everyday sounds identification, go on a listening walk, conduct a sound survey, make a sound map of the school or home, identify items inside of sealed pots or semi-inflated balloons by shaking them and listening, make and explore musical instruments.

- Smelling: go on a smell walk around school, conduct a favourite and least favourite smells survey, identify different smells from unknown smell pots, open a 'smells lab' and make perfume or stink bombs!
- Touching: feel and identify unknown items hidden inside of a mystery bag or box, feel, compare and sort common items and materials according to simple properties, create a feely book or wall (link to the Year 1 'Everyday Materials' topic described on page 75).
- Tasting: taste and compare a range of foods, try new and unfamiliar foods, identify foods whilst blindfolded, conduct a favourite and least favourite tastes survey.

Working scientifically

- **Asking simple questions and recognising that they can be answered in different ways**
- **Observing closely, using simple equipment**
- **Performing simple tests**
- **Identifying and classifying**
- **Using their observations and ideas to suggest answers to questions**
- **Gathering and recording data to help in answering questions**

Animals including Humans in Year 2

> **Statutory Requirement:** notice that animals, including humans, have offspring which grow into adults.

Young children are fascinated to learn about this aspect of biology, particularly in the spring time when the weather is warmer, more food is available and many animals have their babies. Children could visit a local farm to experience a range of new born animals first-hand. There are also opportunities to link with companies which provide schools with eggs, equipment and resources so that children can safely observe animals such as chicks, butterflies, moths, stick insects, ladybirds or silkworms hatching as well as measure them growing over extended periods of time.

Note: If observing frog spawn hatch into tadpoles, please first seek advice on the care and transfer of spawn.

Don't forget to include the birth and growth of human animals by inviting a parent or carer into school with their newborn baby. Encourage children to ask lots of questions as well as to bring baby and toddler photos and memories of themselves into school to share with others.

Working scientifically

- **Asking simple questions and recognising that they can be answered in different ways**
- **Observing closely**
- **Identifying and classifying**

Recording and presenting life cycles

Making and recording observations over periods of time can provide endless possibilities to be innovative and link to other curriculum areas. Taking photos at every stage of an animals' development and then arranging these in chronological order using a scrap book, photo album, flip book, zigzag book, PowerPoint presentation, time-lapse video, diary, display or learning wheel can be great fun as well provide creative opportunities for sequencing.

Children might also use secondary sources such as books and the internet (there are some awesome life cycle videos to be found) as well as ask questions of 'expert' visitors in order to label and describe the different stages in animals' life cycles. There is often tricky, key vocabulary to learn within this topic such as spawn, larva, pupa, cocoon, adult and even metamorphosis!

To further an understanding of the human life cycle, children could watch and discuss time-lapse videos found on the internet which document a child growing and changing over a number of years since birth. Children could use this as a stimulus to present photos of what they looked like as a baby, toddler and child and describe some of the things they could do at each stage of development. To continue the life cycle, encourage children to draw what they think they might look like as a teenager and an adult and also describe what they might be able to do during these future stages. This activity will be extended further in Year 5 when children examine the changes as Humans develop to old age (see page 36).

Working scientifically

- **Gathering and recording data to help in answering questions**
- **Ask people questions and use simple secondary sources to find answers (non-statutory notes and guidance)**

Statutory Requirement: find out about and describe the basic needs of animals, including humans, for survival (water, food and air).

This statutory objective has strong links to another Year 2 biology unit, 'Living Things and their Habitats', whereby children distinguish between things that are living, dead and things that have never been alive by learning about simple characteristics of living things (activities described on page 43).

Children could share their ideas about whether an animal would die or stay alive if it did not: move; breathe; go to the toilet; eat; drink; use their senses; have babies. They should use this information to conclude that all animals need food to eat, water to drink and air to breathe for survival. The scenario of a giant or monster who keeps a human as a pet provides a creative context for children offering advice about what it must do in order to look after the pet human and keep it healthy.

Working scientifically

- **Identifying and classifying**
- **Using their observations and ideas to suggest answers to questions**

Quizzical questions and awesome answers

In order to find out more about the basic needs of animals for survival, encourage children to ask and find answers to survival related questions such as:

- How long can a human survive without food, water or air?
- How many days can a crocodile survive without food?
- Why does a kangaroo rat need to survive without water?
- Why do camels have humps?
- How do animals breathe if they live under water?

Working scientifically

- **Asking simple questions and recognising that they can be answered in different ways**
- **Using their observations and ideas to suggest answers to questions**
- **Ask people questions and use simple secondary sources to find answers (non-statutory notes and guidance)**

> **Statutory Requirement:** describe the importance for humans of exercise, eating the right amounts of different types of food, and hygiene.

Healthy me

Children could keep a 'Healthy me' sticker sheet or diary over a week to record and evaluate their physical activity (including walking to school, riding their bike or scooter and sporty hobbies), the healthy food they have eaten and the frequency of hand washing and teeth cleaning. There are great opportunities here to combine science and mathematics through data handling activities involving simple charts and graphs.

Superhero training school

Another motivating context is to enrol all children in a fictitious 'superhero training school' whereby they aim to become as fit and healthy as possible by the end of the week or topic. Children could undertake an age-related fitness programme such as a circuit of simple exercises each day or skipping and hula hooping at play time. They might even own their own pedometer or fitness watch so that they can calculate the number of steps taken each day. Children should work scientifically by keeping a record of their achievements, tracking improved progress over a specified amount of time. They should use this information to explain the importance of exercise for building strong muscles and bones and to avoid becoming overweight.

Working scientifically

- **Gathering and recording data to help in answering questions**

My healthy plate: sorting food

Children will have learnt earlier in this topic that all animals need food in order to survive. A human could not live for more than a month without food but what does the food we eat actually do for us? Put simply, our food helps us to grow, be active and stay healthy.

Note: Both the Year 2 and Year 3 objectives for this topic require children to understand that we need the right types of food in the right amounts. Teachers should plan together carefully to avoid repetition and ensure a progression from naming and identifying foods in each group to understanding the nutritional value of different foods.

Healthy and unhealthy

Even the youngest children will have some understanding of which foods are healthy and unhealthy for us. Provide them with a large shopping bag or online shopping list containing items to sort according to which they think are healthy and unhealthy choices. A Venn diagram would provide an opportunity for them to consider which items might be placed in the intersection and explain why they think this.

Food groups

Explain to children that all foods can be included in a healthy diet as long as we eat the right amounts of different types of food. In order to get the balance right, we classify food into five different groups: (1) fruit and vegetables; (2) bread, rice, potatoes, cereal and pasta; (3) milk and dairy; (4) meat, fish, eggs and beans; (5) food and drink high in fat/sugar. Provide them with labels for the five food groups and invite children to re-sort the original shopping items according to food type and take photographs to keep as a permanent record.

How much?

A simple way to demonstrate how much of each type of food we should eat is to create a huge triangle on the table-top or floor using string or coloured tape and divide this into four horizontal zones, starting with: 'bread, rice, potatoes, cereal and pasta' at the base of the triangle then 'fruits and vegetables' in the second zone. Above this comes 'milk and dairy foods' together with 'meat, fish, eggs and beans' in the third zone and finally 'foods high in fat/sugar' at the top of the triangle.

Ensure children understand that the balance should be applied to food eaten over a day or even a week rather than every meal they eat. They could keep a food diary and then group and classify the foods they have eaten using the triangle (pyramid) model. Are they eating a healthy and balanced diet? Can they use this information to evaluate whether or not they are eating the right amount of different types of food? Don't forget to take photographs as evidence!

You are what you eat

Children will have great fun drawing around each other on a roll of plain wallpaper and then selecting and sticking images of different types of food to represent acceptable or poor food choices. An unhealthy person might have doughnut eyes, chips for hair, a pizza stomach and chocolate biscuit feet! A healthy person might have broccoli hair, grape finger nails, fish thighs, yoghurt knee caps and potato feet! Children should remember that a small number of items from the top of the food pyramid should be included in a healthy diet.

Another creative way to link healthy food choices to the art curriculum is for children to learn about the work of Italian painter, Giuseppe Arcimboldo, best known for creating imaginative portraits using objects such as fruits and vegetables.

Working scientifically
- **Identifying and classifying**
- **Gathering and recording data to help in answering questions**

Learning about hygiene: germs

Squirt some sanitising gel followed by plenty of glitter onto the hands of a willing volunteer and ask them to rub their hands together until the glitter is evenly spread. The glitter represents the usually invisible germs we have on our hands every day. This child should shake hands with a range of children and touch different surfaces around the classroom. The glitter is a great visual representation of how quickly and easily germs on our hands are spread between us. Children should understand that washing our hands with soap is one of the most important things we can do to avoid spreading germs to others.

How does soap help to get rid of germs?

Create a model to help children visualise what happens to germs when we wash our hands with and without soap. They should pour water into a small bowl and then sprinkle a light covering of black pepper onto the water to represent germs on the surface of our skin. Children could compare what happens when they dip one finger into the centre of the peppered water and then again with a different finger covered in washing-up liquid. In the second instance they will observe the pepper 'germs' moving quickly away from their finger as they are being repelled by the soap.

What happens when you eat without washing your hands?

Start with a loaf of fresh white bread. Take one slice using tweezers, being careful not to touch this with your hands, and place this into a clear, sealable bag. Next, wash your hands thoroughly before placing a second slice of bread into another bag. Finally, pass a third piece of bread around the class so that every child can handle it before placing this into another bag. Label the bags and seal them tightly. Over an extended period of time, children will observe that mould grows on each sample but much sooner and in greater amounts on the slice that had been passed around. This is a powerful way for children to understand that, even though their hands might look clean, we must always wash the germs off before we handle food.

Brush your teeth!

Children could investigate how different kinds of drinks affect their teeth by using clean egg shells as a close substitute for real teeth and suspending these in cups containing different types of drinks (such as water, cola, diet cola, fresh orange, apple juice and fizzy flavoured water). After a week, children should use a hand lens, digital microscope or visualiser to examine the egg shells carefully and make decisions about which drinks are most harmful to our teeth and why it is so important to brush them properly and regularly. Children might conduct a further investigation to see whether it is possible to protect the egg shell 'tooth' from an unhealthy drink by first coating it with toothpaste or mouthwash.

Animals including Humans in Year 3

Statutory Requirement: identify that animals, including humans, need the right types and amount of nutrition, and that they cannot make their own food; they get nutrition from what they eat.

It is vital that Year 3 teachers simply do not repeat 'Healthy plate' activities covered in Year 2 (described on page 26) and ensure that there is adequate progression in knowledge and understanding by linking aspects of food choice to nutrition.

Reading and comparing nutrition labels

The majority of pre-packed foods in the UK provide some nutritional information on the label and this can help us to choose a healthy and varied diet. Most children will find it easier to understand the red (high), amber (medium) and green (low) colour coding system on the front of many packs and use these to make comparisons between foods. Remember, it is okay to choose 'red/amber' foods for an occasional treat but it would be better to eat 'green' foods regularly. More able children could examine the nutrition information provided on a range of different foods and use this to sort, group and rank food according to the amount of energy, fat or a nutrient provided per 100 g.

Nutrition calculators

Children will enjoy using secondary sources of information to calculate their own estimated daily calorie intake. Many big brand coffee shops, fast food providers and restaurants provide free online nutrition calculators or apps and these can be used to research the nutritional value of their favourite treats – often with quite alarming results!

> ### Working scientifically
> - **Gathering, recording, classifying and presenting data in a variety of ways to help in answering questions**
> - **Recording findings using simple scientific language, drawings, labelled diagrams, keys, bar charts and tables**
> - **Recognise when and how secondary sources might help them to answer questions that cannot be answered through practical investigations (non-statutory notes and guidance)**

How much fat?

Children should understand that fats must be included in a balanced diet and are required for our bodies to store energy and our brains to work well, however, not all fats are healthy. They will observe that food nutrition labels subdivide fats into 'unsaturated' (shown to be beneficial to our health) and 'saturated' (associated with poor health).

Saturated fats in foods can be greasy and are easily identified by placing a specified amount of different foods onto brown paper and observing the size of the grease stain produced. Some children could make a quantitative measurement of the area of the stain using centimetre squared paper. The results of this investigation could be compared to nutritional data regarding fat content on food labels – do the numbers agree with children's grease stain evidence?

- **Setting up simple practical enquiries, comparative and fair tests**
- **Making systematic and careful observations and, where appropriate, taking accurate measurements using standard units, using a range of equipment, including thermometers and data loggers**
- **Gathering, recording, classifying and presenting data in a variety of ways to help in answering questions**

How much sugar?

In addition to scrutinising food labels, children could contact organisations such as The British Dental Health Foundation to obtain information regarding the amount of sugar found in common foods and drinks or download and use a simple 'sugar smart app' which works on an electronic device as a bar code scanner. A visual display of product labels with the equivalent number of teaspoons of sugar (presented in clear, sealable bags) or sugar cubes per 100 g makes a hard hitting presentation of this information.

Working scientifically

- **Gathering, recording, classifying and presenting data in a variety of ways to help in answering questions**
- **Recording findings using simple scientific language, drawings, labelled diagrams, keys, bar charts and tables**
- **Recognise when and how secondary sources might help them to answer questions that cannot be answered through practical investigations (non-statutory notes and guidance)**

Five-a-day

Children should understand that fruit and vegetables are an important part of a healthy, balanced diet as they are usually low in fat and calories, and provide nutrients such as vitamins and minerals that can help us to look after our body. Children could use secondary sources to find out more about the 'five-a-day' campaign including the acceptable portion size of 80 g. They could count, measure and cut real fruit and vegetables (from a variety provided) to be photographed and used in their own informative poster campaign.

Working scientifically

- **Gathering, recording, classifying and presenting data in a variety of ways to help in answering questions**
- **Recognise when and how secondary sources might help them to answer questions that cannot be answered through practical investigations (non-statutory notes and guidance)**

Creative x-rays

There are some very believable x-ray apps (cameras, effects and scanners) that can be downloaded for free and used creatively for children to predict and then 'see for themselves' what different bones in their body look like. Ask if they can name any of these bones and suggest which bones protect softer parts of our bodies such as our brain, nerves in the spinal column, lungs, heart, kidneys, liver and bladder.

For some extra fun, you could even pretend to x-ray a range of animal soft toys to show what their skeletons look like on screen (you will need to prepare a PowerPoint presentation with corresponding animal x-ray images in advance). Put the animal toy in a large box (classroom x-ray machine) and click to advance the presentation to the relevant slide. Children could observe how animal skeletons differ from humans as well as each other and also learn that some animals, such as starfish or worms, have no internal skeleton made of bone (as long as you have these toys to include in the activity).

Working scientifically

- **Reporting on findings from enquiries, including oral and written explanations, displays or presentations of results and conclusions**
- **Using straightforward scientific evidence to answer questions or to support their findings**

Bones for protection

Anatomical models can be expensive to buy so challenge children to get creative by thinking about which everyday objects and materials they could use to represent the brain (play-dough, marshmallows, jelly – you can actually buy brain shaped jelly moulds on the internet!) and then what might represent the rigid skull that surrounds and protects this (paper mâché or plaster of Paris left to set around a curved balloon, a cycling helmet, the hard shell from an egg protecting the soft, runny yolk). There are no right or wrong answers to the challenge; the aim is for children to consider how our bones can be important for protection.

Bones for support

Give each child a thin rubber glove to represent the human hand and observe how, without bones, the hand is floppy and unsupported. They could use five drinking straws, one inserted into each finger of the glove, to show how the 'hand' now has a structure of bones and can be supported easily.

Working scientifically

- **Gathering, recording, classifying and presenting data in a variety of ways to help in answering questions**
- **Using straightforward scientific evidence to answer questions or to support their findings**

Muscles for movement

Ask children to draw around one hand onto card and cut this out. With a pencil, they should mark where their cardboard fingers would bend (where their joints are) and make horizontal creases in these places. They should cut drinking straws into small pieces – just long enough to represent the bones in between our joints and then carefully stick each one in place with thin pre-cut strips of tape.

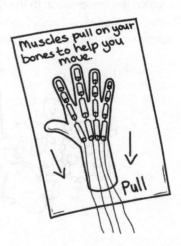

Children should cut five lengths of string (one for each finger) to be threaded through the straws and taped down on the underside of the tip of each finger. The string represents how muscles are attached to our bones. They can stick their 'hand' onto card and try pulling the strings to see how muscles and bones work together to enable us to move.

Working scientifically

- **Gathering, recording, classifying and presenting data in a variety of ways to help in answering questions**
- **Using straightforward scientific evidence to answer questions or to support their findings**

Animals including Humans in Year 4

> **Statutory Requirement:** describe the simple functions of the basic parts of the digestive system in humans.

Human digestive system

Making a 'working' model of the human digestive system is one of the activities primary children will talk about and remember for years and years! Children love anything a bit gross or related to bodily functions and so tracking the journey of a piece of food as it travels through the digestive system is an activity they will enjoy recounting with detail. Here are some ideas for how to model this but, of course, children should suggest their own ideas too:

1. **Mouth:** Begin with food such as a banana and a plain biscuit. Put these into a small bowl to represent the mouth and mash the food with a fork to represent the teeth chopping food into tiny pieces (a mortar and pestle also works well here to represent mouth and teeth) and the rounded side of a spoon to represent the tongue. Add a small amount of water to the bowl to represent the saliva in our mouths which helps to make food easier to swallow.

2. **Oesophagus:** Use a 25 cm length of flexible plastic tubing such as pipe insulation (diameter of at least 3 cm) to represent the food pipe which connects our throat with our stomach. Food is pushed down the oesophagus so children should continuously squeeze the tubing to represent this action.

3. **Stomach:** Deposit the squeezed food into a clear sandwich bag to represent the stomach where food is stored. Add a small amount of lemon juice to represent digestive juice called stomach acid and seal the bag to represent the valve to the stomach closing. Squash and squeeze the contents of the bag to mix it up and mimic the action of our stomach walls breaking down food.

4. **Small intestine:** Cut a small hole in the corner of the clear bag and empty the food slowly into one leg of a pair of sheer tights to represent the small intestine. Make sure you do this over an empty tray as the action of squeezing the food through the intestine will release liquid from the food and this can be collected in the tray below. The liquid represents digested nutrients absorbed through the intestinal walls which are useful to us for growth and energy and are then transported throughout our body.

5. **Large intestine and rectum:** Cut the toe off the tights and squeeze the remaining food into a paper cup. This represents our body getting rid of the undigested parts of food that we do not need by pushing this through the large intestine (foot of the tights) and into the rectum (cup) where it is stored.

6. **Anus:** Use a thick pencil to push a small hole into the bottom of the paper cup (where the waste food is being stored). Get another cup and put this inside of the original cup and push down so that the waste food comes out of the hole. This will represent how waste food leaves our body through the anus when we use the toilet.

> Working scientifically
> - **Gathering, recording, classifying and presenting data in a variety of ways to help in answering questions**
> - **Recording findings using simple scientific language, drawings, labelled diagrams, keys, bar charts and tables**
> - **Using straightforward scientific evidence to answer questions or to support their findings**

Digestive system measuring

There are some staggering measurements to be made when learning about the human digestive system. Children could research this and link with the Year 4 mathematics curriculum to estimate, compare and calculate different standard measures as well as convert between different units of measure. They could measure and cut string to compare lengths relating to facts such as:

- The oesophagus is about 25 cm long in adults.

- The small intestine is around 6.5 m long! It fits inside your body all wrapped up.
- The large intestine is around 1.5 m long! It is called the large intestine (even though it is shorter in length than the small intestine) because it is much larger in diameter.

> **Working scientifically**
>
> - **Making systematic and careful observations and, where appropriate, taking accurate measurements using standard units, using a range of equipment, including thermometers and data loggers**
> - **Recording findings using simple scientific language, drawings, labelled diagrams, keys, bar charts and tables**
> - **Recognise when and how secondary sources might help them to answer questions that cannot be answered through practical investigations (non-statutory notes and guidance)**

> **Statutory Requirement:** identify the different types of teeth in humans and their simple functions.

Open wide

Each child should spend a few minutes feeling around their teeth with their tongue or a finger and also examining their teeth in a mirror. They should try and count how many teeth they have and think about whether all teeth look and feel the same. Using red and white play-dough (or coloured salt dough), challenge children to make a model of a full set of human teeth (top and bottom jaw). How can they make the molar teeth at the back look flat, bumpy and perfect for chewing food? Also, the canine teeth nearer the front look sharp, pointed and perfect for tearing food and the incisor teeth at the front look flat, chiselled and perfect for biting food?

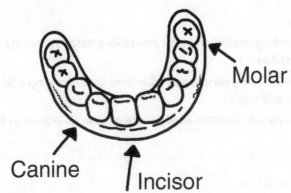

Molar

Canine

Incisor

Working scientifically
- **Making systematic and careful observations**
- **Recording findings using simple scientific language, drawings, labelled diagrams, keys, bar charts and tables**

Take a bite

Give children a selection of food to eat and ask them to identify which teeth they are using and why. Examples might include an apple or biscuit to cut into (incisors for biting), a crusty baguette or deep crust pizza to rip a piece off (canines for tearing) and some jelly sweets or grapes to chew (molars for grinding).

Can children think of equipment or utensils found in the kitchen to represent different kinds of teeth? They might suggest a flat, bumpy potato masher for a molar or a sharp, pointed kitchen knife for a canine and a flat, square bladed cheese or butter knife for an incisor tooth.

Working scientifically

- **Gathering, recording, classifying and presenting data in a variety of ways to help in answering questions**
- **Identifying differences, similarities or changes related to simple scientific ideas and processes**

Statutory Requirement: construct and interpret a variety of food chains, identifying producers, predators and prey.

Food chain activities in Year 4 should carry on from prior learning in the Year 2 'Living Things and their Habitats' topic during which children describe how animals obtain their food from plants and other animals using the idea of a simple food chain.

Year 4 children could begin with a more sophisticated version of the game 'Find it and eat it!' (described on page 47) whereby they are given either an animal or plant picture card and then have to find and join with other children in order to make a plausible food chain. Each chain must begin with a green plant (the producer in the chain) and should continue in order of 'what is eaten by what?' Challenge teams to see who can make the longest food chain and correctly identify producers, predators and prey.

Presenting food chains

An ingenious way for children to present the food chains they have researched and devised is for them to draw and write the name of each plant or animal in the chain on a separate upturned paper or polystyrene cup. They should start with the 'plant cup' (the producer in the chain) and then stack the remaining cups on top of this in order of 'what is eaten by what'. Encourage children to make a loud chomping noise each time they stack a cup to show how this animal is eating the previous one. They could also write key vocabulary on each cup to show which plants/animals are producers, predators or prey in the chain. Additional challenge can be given by asking children to think of a food chain that contains at least five different animals or one that includes a human.

- **Asking relevant questions and using different types of scientific enquiries to answer them**
- **Gathering, recording, classifying and presenting data in a variety of ways to help in answering questions**
- **Recording findings using simple scientific language, drawings, labelled diagrams, keys, bar charts and tables**

Exploring owl pellets

A real-life opportunity for children to learn about food chains is for them to explore the undigested parts of an owl's food which have been ejected through the mouth. These pellets have not passed through the owl's intestines and so are hardly affected by digestion and safe to explore. Children should tease them apart carefully using tweezers or cocktail sticks once they have been soaked for about 30 minutes in water. Some of the things that might be found hidden within owl pellets are the bones of birds, mammals and fish, teeth, claws, beaks, feathers, insect parts and seed husks, therefore, they can tell us precisely what prey these predators have been feeding on.

Further information on how to buy, store, use and analyse owl pellets can be found on various internet sites including the Barn Owl Trust.

- **Setting up simple practical enquiries, comparative and fair tests**
- **Making systematic and careful observations**

Animals including Humans in Year 5

Statutory Requirement: describe the changes as humans develop to old age.

Learning about life cycles begins in Year 2 when children notice that animals, including humans, have offspring which grow into adults (activities described on page 23). To further their understanding of what happens to humans as they develop to old age, children could invite a grandparent or older friend of the school to talk to them about the changes that take place in later years. They could also compare photographs which document birth, childhood, adolescence, adulthood and old age and prepare questions to ask an older person at home, in their own family or a close friend or neighbour.

There are some excellent video clips (time-lapse photographs or face-morph progression) to be found on the internet and these can help children to observe and discuss changes over time using secondary sources. Finally, they could upload current photographs of themselves to a free ageing app which will show (in a rather crude way) what individual children might look like in later years. They could prepare a commentary to accompany the resulting image, describing the changes that have taken place and their implications.

- **Reporting and presenting findings from enquiries, including conclusions, causal relationships and explanations of and degree of trust in results, in oral and written forms such as displays and other presentations**
- **Identifying scientific evidence that has been used to support or refute ideas or arguments**

Animals including Humans in Year 6

Statutory Requirement: identify and name the main parts of the human circulatory system, and describe the functions of the heart, blood vessels and blood.

What's the link?

Begin with a series of images to include a bicycle pump (heart pumps blood around body), athlete (healthy heart), upside down pear (shape of the human heart), cupid (heart signifying love), stethoscope (listening to the heart), vampire (feeding on blood), hospital blood bank, industrial valve (valves open and close to the heart), delivery van (delivery system) etc and ask children to discuss what the images might have in common. Explain that the circulatory system is the body's delivery system and helps us to understand the important jobs of our blood, blood vessels and heart as blood is moved (circulated) around our body.

Working scientifically

- **Identifying scientific evidence that has been used to support or refute ideas or arguments**

Learning about the heart

Children should learn that the heart works like a pump (or two pumps in one) sending blood to every part of your body carrying the oxygen and nutrients that it needs, it also then pumps blood back again with the waste that your body does not need. They could make a simple working model to show how the heart sends blood around the body by half filling a clear beaker with red water, cutting the neck off a balloon then stretching the remaining rubber over the rim of the beaker. They should make one tiny snip with scissors in the centre of the stretched balloon skin and push a drinking straw through so that the balloon seals tightly around the straw and the lower end is submerged into the water.

To demonstrate their model, children should place the beaker in a tray and then start 'pumping' the 'heart' by pressing down on the stretched balloon skin and releasing again. Children should understand that before your heart beats, it fills with blood (red water in the beaker), and then it squeezes (press on the balloon) to squirt the blood along special tubes called arteries that carry blood away from the heart and around your body (liquid coming out of the straw). They should observe that blood does not travel in a continuous, smooth flow; rather it is pushed in a steady pulse as special valves open and close. Children could demonstrate their models accompanied by an oral commentary of what the heart is and its part in the circulatory system.

Working scientifically

- **Recording data and results of increasing complexity using scientific diagrams and labels, classification keys, tables, scatter graphs, bar and line graphs**
- **Reporting and presenting findings from enquiries, including conclusions, causal relationships and explanations of and degree of trust in results, in oral and written forms such as displays and other presentations**

Blood vessels: articulate through art

Search the internet for a magnified image (coloured scanning electron micrograph) of blood vessels in the human body and show this to children without telling them what they are looking at. Ask them to describe what they can see (not what they think the image is) and build up a creative, imaginary class poem using detailed descriptions such as:

- 'an old withered tree with gnarled branches stretching for miles'
- 'an underground network of roots'
- 'a technicoloured map leading to distant places'

Now focus on suggestions of what the image might actually be, taking ideas from children, before explaining that they have been looking at millions of narrow tubes found all around our bodies called blood vessels. Discuss how the blood vessels that carry blood rich in oxygen away from the heart are called arteries and the ones that carry deoxygenated blood back to the heart are called veins.

Children should understand that, although many books and scientific diagrams show arteries as red blood vessels and veins as blue blood vessels, this is just a way of differentiating between the two types. All blood is red (oxygen-rich blood is bright red as it leaves the heart whilst deoxygenated blood is dark red) and some veins close to the skin's surface only appear blue due to the effect of looking at them through our skin. Children could produce a life size figure by drawing around someone in the class on a roll of plain wallpaper and then sticking on images of the heart and lungs in the correct positions. They could use runny red and blue paint and blow this through a straw so that is reaches every part of the body. This gives the effect of millions of blood vessels branching out like tiny tubes in every direction.

Working scientifically

- **Recording data and results of increasing complexity using scientific diagrams and labels, classification keys, tables, scatter graphs, bar and line graphs**

Learning about the circulatory system

A drama or role play where different children take the parts of the heart, lungs, blood cells and body parts is a great way for them to physically and verbally explain the different processes in the circulatory system. Children could devise a bus timetable and then write and perform a creative commentary around the circulatory system as the tour guide of this unusual excursion. Asking them to sign their names next to key words (such as: heart, lungs, oxygen, blood vessels, arteries, veins, blood cells) on a list provided is a great incentive for children to include key scientific vocabulary in their scripts.

Working scientifically

- **Reporting and presenting findings from enquiries, including conclusions, causal relationships and explanations of and degree of trust in results, in oral and written forms such as displays and other presentations**

Circulatory system measuring

Children will have fun using secondary sources to research and then calculate some of the staggering statistics and measurements linked to the human circulatory system. There are excellent links here with the Year 6 mathematics curriculum whereby children read, write, order and compare numbers up to 10,000,000 and also convert between miles and kilometres.

For example, they could find out approximately how long our system of blood vessels is or how much blood is pumped through the body every day as well as measure and calculate how many times the average heart beats in one week.

Working scientifically

- **Taking measurements, using a range of scientific equipment, with increasing accuracy and precision, taking repeat readings when appropriate**
- **Recognise which secondary sources will be most useful to research their ideas and begin to separate opinion from fact (non-statutory notes and guidance)**

> **Statutory Requirement:** recognise the impact of diet, exercise, drugs and lifestyle on the way their bodies function.

Year 6 teachers should follow on from activities taught during Year 2 whereby children learn the importance for humans of exercise, eating the right amounts of different types of food, and hygiene (described on page 26) and in Year 3 when they learn that we need the right types and amount of nutrition (described on page 29).

There are excellent links to the personal, social and health curriculum during this topic and teachers may wish to follow a scheme of work or programme of study already in place for teaching children about diet, exercise, drugs and lifestyle.

Healthy me

Children could keep a journal or diary over a number of weeks in order to record, interpret and evaluate lifestyle choices. They might use the data collected to calculate:

1 the average number of hours spent playing on electronic games, devices or computers
2 the average number of hours spent watching television per week
3 the average number of hours spent doing sport or physical hobbies per week
4 the average number of hours spent sleeping per night
5 the average number of steps taken per day (using a pedometer or fitness watch)

There are great opportunities here for combining science and mathematics through data handling. Children could look for patterns in data in an attempt to identify causal relationships between two or more variables.

> ### Working scientifically
> - **Taking measurements, using a range of scientific equipment, with increasing accuracy and precision, taking repeat readings when appropriate**
> - **Recording data and results of increasing complexity using scientific diagrams and labels, classification keys, tables, scatter graphs, bar and line graphs**
> - **Reporting and presenting findings from enquiries, including conclusions, causal relationships and explanations of and degree of trust in results, in oral and written forms such as displays and other presentations**

Investigating the effects of exercise on pulse rate

Ask children to locate where they can feel the pulse in different parts of their body (some possibilities are inside of the wrist, side of the neck, side of the temples, inside of the elbow and behind the knee). If possible, they could examine different pieces of equipment used for measuring heart rate, such as a stethoscope, pulse meter and commercial products such as a 'smart heart' monitor and accompanying app.

Children could use equipment or simple counting to calculate their own pulse rate and then the effects on this with exercise. They could plan and perform their own daily or weekly fitness circuit, including specially chosen exercises to target different muscle groups including cardiovascular aimed at raising heart rate. They should use these opportunities to measure, record and evaluate increased fitness over time as well as investigate recovery rates.

> ### Working scientifically
> - **Planning different types of scientific enquiries to answer questions, including recognising and controlling variables where necessary**
> - **Taking measurements, using a range of scientific equipment, with increasing accuracy and precision, taking repeat readings when appropriate**

- **Recording data and results of increasing complexity using scientific diagrams and labels, classification keys, tables, scatter graphs, bar and line graphs**
- **Reporting and presenting findings from enquiries, including conclusions, causal relationships and explanations of and degree of trust in results, in oral and written forms such as displays and other presentations**

A responsible task

Children in Year 6 could be given the responsibility of organising and running a healthy school tuck shop at break times. They will need to decide which snacks and drinks should be sold in the shop by researching nutritional information and using 'sugar smart' apps to either confirm or rule out a range of possibilities from the stock list. Children will also enjoy researching, planning and preparing a range of healthy snacks to sell in the shop by following nutritional recipes, such as: fruit kebabs, healthy smoothies, granola bars and frozen yoghurts.

Working scientifically

- **Reporting and presenting findings from enquiries, including conclusions, causal relationships and explanations of and degree of trust in results, in oral and written forms such as displays and other presentations**
- **Recognise which secondary sources will be most useful to research their ideas and begin to separate opinion from fact (non-statutory notes and guidance)**

The impact of smoking: a model

Secure a piece of light coloured sponge with an elastic band to the inside of the hinged lid of a glass pasta or sweets jar. Roll a piece of newspaper up into a cigarette shape and set this on fire using a safety lighter before dropping the lit paper into the jar and closing the lid. Leave the paper to burn for up to eight minutes to represent the average time it takes to smoke a cigarette. Lift the lid of the jar and observe that there is still plenty of smoke trapped inside.

Repeat this procedure over a number of hours to represent how an average smoker has 15 cigarettes a day. Remove and carefully examine the sponge as well as the contents of the jar, both of which represent the tar and nicotine that is left in a smoker's lungs every day. Children should form their own conclusions about how this model is similar or different to the effects of smoking on a person's lungs and the implications of this on their health.

Working scientifically

- **Reporting and presenting findings from enquiries, including conclusions, causal relationships and explanations of and degree of trust in results, in oral and written forms such as displays and other presentations**

- **Identifying scientific evidence that has been used to support or refute ideas or arguments**

> **Statutory Requirement:** describe the ways in which nutrients and water are transported within animals, including humans.

It might be a good idea to recap the human digestive system from the Year 4 programme of study (described on page 32), in particular the part of the model where food travels through the small intestine (one leg of a pair of sheer tights) and liquid is released to represent water and digested nutrients being absorbed through the intestinal walls. Children should understand that water and nutrients which have been transported throughout our body in our bloodstream are useful to us for growth and energy.

Learning more about blood

Children will learn more about how blood is essential for good health by making a model of a sample of blood. At each stage of this activity, they should compare the items they are adding with magnified images of the real ingredients (found easily on the internet).

1   First, they should add water and two drops of yellow food colouring to a small plastic bottle (enough to half fill the bottle) to represent plasma, which is mostly water absorbed from the intestines from what we eat and drink. Plasma carries things like nutrients around our body and so children could add a sprinkle of salt to their liquid to represent minerals found in plasma.

2   Red blood cells carry oxygen all around our body. They are the most plentiful type of cell in blood and that is why blood appears the colour of red. Children can represent this by mixing Cheerios with red food colouring in a clear, sealable bag until the cereal turns red. They should observe that, when these are added to the plasma in their bottle, it will turn red too.

3   Children can represent white blood cells by adding a small number of white marshmallows or small white pompoms to the sample and learn that these help us to fight infections. White blood cells are bigger than red blood cells and there are not too many of these found in our blood when we are healthy but once we get sick, our body makes more to protect us.

4   Children could represent platelets found in our blood by adding large raisins to the sample to represent the tiny round cells that will help us to stop bleeding if we get cut.

Children could photograph their models and annotate these to explain how different ingredients in blood have special functions. They should make particular reference to how blood transports nutrients and water around our bodies.

Working scientifically
- **Recording data and results of increasing complexity using scientific diagrams and labels, classification keys, tables, scatter graphs, bar and line graphs**
- **Reporting and presenting findings from enquiries, including conclusions, causal relationships and explanations of and degree of trust in results, in oral and written forms such as displays and other presentations**

3
A Creative Approach to Teaching Living Things and their Habitats

Children throughout the primary age range should have plenty of opportunities to go hunting and searching outside in different local habitats such as the school grounds, park, woodland or sea shore if at all possible at different times of the year. They should be able to observe plants and animals first-hand and consider why living things are suited to the environment in which they are discovered.

Living Things and their Habitats in Year 2

Children in Year 2 should begin with an appreciation of what it means to be alive before they progress to distinguishing between living, once living and non-living things. A fun way to introduce this concept is to compare a large doll or puppet with a real child from the class. Ask children to think carefully about what the real child can do that the doll/puppet child cannot do. This is an excellent way to get children thinking about basic characteristics of living things such as breathing, eating and drinking, changing and growing, moving (by yourself), using the five senses, going to the toilet and possibly having babies when an adult. Children will develop an understanding of how something that is alive can do all of these things whereas a non-living thing cannot do any of these things by itself.

Note: Some children might say that the real child can talk or cry, however, this is not a characteristic that ensures that something is alive or not.

Extend the activity to all living things and ask children to compare an animal with a plant. Young children might struggle with the fact that plants are living things too and that they breathe (take in and get rid of gases), eat and drink (absorb nutrients and water from soil), change and grow, move (turn towards the light is a good example of this), go to the toilet (get rid of waste gases) and have babies (produce seeds that grow into new plants). As long as children understand that plants feed, grow and change then this is a good starting point for this age group.

Working scientifically
- **Identifying and classifying**
- **Using their observations and ideas to suggest answers to questions**

Sorting and grouping

Asking children to sort a range of real objects or picture cards is an excellent way of ascertaining what they understand about living things. Examples to include could be: cat; healthy plant growing in a pot; apple growing on a tree; newborn baby; older person; bird; fish; fire; plastic building block; doll; battery-powered moving toy; jack-in-a-box; fake spider; artificial flower; inflated balloon; shoe; banana; tooth; bone; wooden lolly stick; ball of wool; newspaper; fallen brown leaf.

Begin by providing each pair or group with two hoops and challenging them to classify and sort the items into only living and non-living. Take photographs of the sorted hoops as evidence of their initial understanding. Choose one of the items such as a ball of wool and look confused. Ask children where the wool has come from and discuss how it was once part of a sheep, growing and changing. Explain how the wool was once alive but is no longer living since it has been removed from the sheep. Scaffold children's understanding of how the two hoops can be overlapped and a new category introduced which has characteristics of both living and non-living – we will call this new category: once alive or dead.

Ask children to re-sort their items considering which ones would now move into the intersection of the hoops and explain why they think this. Take a second photograph of this as evidence of progress in conceptual understanding.

Hunting and searching

Children love going on welly walks, scavenger hunts or thinking trails and these are all excellent ways for them to identify and classify living, once living (dead) and non-living things in their local environment. They should take plenty of photographs as evidence of what they have found.

Note: Many young children will think that deciduous trees that have lost their leaves in winter are dead and no longer growing.

> Working scientifically
> - **Identifying and classifying**
> - **Using their observations and ideas to suggest answers to questions**
> - **Gathering and recording data to help in answering questions**

The activities described in this section should progress from those carried out in the Year 1 'Plants' topic whereby children identify and name a variety of common wild and garden plants, including deciduous and evergreen trees (see page 7).

Out and about

A quick internet search will lead you to a wide range of resources available to support young children in identifying and naming common plants, such as flowers, leaves, twigs and trees, as well as animals including minibeasts and birds. Particular favourites of mine are the iDials and spotter sheets that can be downloaded free from the Nature Detectives website (Woodland Trust) and used easily by children. Alternatively a simple 'I-spy' sheet can be created with labelled photographs prior to the adventure.

Terrific trees

Trees in the school grounds could be labelled after identification so that other children can enjoy this information too. An extension of this is to include the age of a tree by measuring one metre up from the ground and then around the trunk at this point. The teacher can help with a quick calculation by dividing this measurement by 2.5 (for trees found in an open space such as school grounds). This will give children a rough guide to how many years old each tree is.

Articulate through art

There are some fantastic art projects for children that can be utilised when identifying and naming common plants, in particular flowering plants. A study of the work of American artist Georgia O'Keeffe, best known for her paintings of enlarged flowers, can provide a stunning opportunity for children to articulate their understanding through large scale observational drawing and painting.

> Working scientifically
> - **Observing closely, using simple equipment**
> - **Identifying and classifying**
> - **Gathering and recording data to help in answering questions**
> - **Ask people questions and use simple secondary sources to find answers (non-statutory guidance)**

> **Statutory Requirement:** identify that most living things live in habitats to which they are suited and describe how different habitats provide for the basic needs of different kinds of animals and plants, and how they depend on each other.

This objective could be enjoyed alongside the one described prior to this as it is imperative that children gain first-hand experience of exploring plants and animals in their natural habitats across the school year. Children could investigate, for example, why woodlice are found under logs and stones, why herring gulls are found at the beach, why most mushrooms are found growing in damp conditions and why some plants, such as snowdrops, prefer to grow in dappled shade.

Children could also set up and observe real-life examples of habitats such as a bug hotel or bird box in the school grounds as well as a wormery or wood lice choice chamber in their classroom. They should make observations over time and gain exciting first-hand experience of how different habitats provide the basic needs of different kinds of animals and plants.

Working scientifically

- **Observing closely, using simple equipment**
- **Identifying and classifying**
- **Ask people questions and use simple secondary sources to find answers (non-statutory guidance)**

Post box problem

It is interesting for children to find out about habitats that are further afield such as rainforests, deserts, polar-regions and oceans. Present them with a collection of large envelopes that have been left behind in the post box. Share the unusual addresses written on the envelopes and ask children to suggest a plant or animal that might be suited to each one. Addresses could include:

- Allotment Place, Log Pile Lane, Stones End
- The Lily Pad, School Pond, Learning Lane
- Sandy Ridge, Desert Drive, Heat Highway
- The Undercurrent, Salty Shores, Ocean Drive
- Tree Tops, Rain Forest Road, Tropical Town
- Igloo Avenue, Ice cap Ridge, Arctic Way
- Leafy Burrow, Gran's Garden, Green Grass Gates
- Oak Wood Walk, Sycamore Street, Mossy Way

Extend children's thinking and discussion to include a consideration of why these plants or animals are suited to each habitat, such as why would a frog live in a pond or why might a camel live in a desert as well as why would you not find an oak tree in the Arctic? There are excellent links here with the children's book *Meerkat Mail* by Emily Gravett. Children could extend their writing skills by creating letters or postcards from animals living in one habitat to another.

- **Identifying and classifying**
- **Using their observations and ideas to suggest answers to questions**

Make a habitat in a box

Children could research the plants and animals found living in each type of habitat described on the envelopes in the 'Post box problem' activity. A fun and creative way for them to record their findings is to decorate the inside of a shoebox as if it were the habitat itself. Children can then either draw or cut and stick pictures as well as place models of plants and animals inside of their box to show which you would find in each type of environment. This activity has excellent links with the design and technology, art and geography curricula too.

Working scientifically

- **Identifying and classifying**
- **Gathering and recording data to help in answering questions**
- **Ask people questions and use simple secondary sources to find answers (non-statutory guidance)**

> **Statutory Requirement:** describe how animals obtain their food from plants and other animals, using the idea of a simple food chain, and identify and name different sources of food.

In Year 2, children will begin to learn about simple food chains. Their knowledge and understanding will be extended in the Year 4 'Animals including Humans' topic as described on page 32.

Find it and eat it!

Make picture cards and sort them into Group A (rabbit, mouse, crab, caterpillar, ant, worm, snail, cow, zebra, giraffe) and Group B (grass, grass, grass, grass, grain, leaf, leaf, carrot, dandelion, seaweed, blue tit, duck, seagull, robin, owl, fox, leopard, lion, human). Begin by giving a third of the class an animal picture card from Group A and the remainder of the class an assortment of plant and animal picture cards from Group B.

All of the children should move around the room before asking the Group A animals to find a plant that they would eat and then also an animal that would eat them! Once they have formed a reasonable trio or team, children must stand in order of what 'is eaten by' what, for example the leaf comes first in line as it 'is eaten by' the worm which 'is eaten by' the bird. Ask children to link arms to form a chain and explain that we can show feeding relationships in this way called a food chain.

Working scientifically

- **Identifying and classifying**
- **Using their observations and ideas to suggest answers to questions**

Research it!

It might seem like a straightforward question but when children ask, 'What does an antelope eat?' or 'What does a hedgehog eat?' being able to use secondary sources for information can be your saving grace! Giving children time to research what different animals eat will enable them to formulate their own food chains of a much higher quality. An internet search using the question frame: 'What does a ... eat?' is a simple way for them to gather a range of suggestions and then record, adapt and refine their own food chains.

> Working scientifically
> - **Ask people questions and use simple secondary sources to find answers (non-statutory guidance)**

Food chain paper chain

Give children a number of pre-cut strips of paper (30 cm x 6 cm) and explain that they are going to make a 'food chain paper chain' to present the most impressive food chain that they have researched and formulated. They should draw the plant and animals in their chain on separate strips of paper then link and glue these together in the correct order to make a chain. Completed chains look impressive as part of a classroom display, hanging as a colourful border or from the ceiling.

> Working scientifically
> - **Identifying and classifying**
> - **Gathering and recording data to help in answering questions**

Living Things and their Habitats in Year 4

Statutory Requirement: recognise that living things can be grouped in a variety of ways.

Human classification

Start with some whole-class 'human classification' whereby children have to sort themselves into groups by looking carefully at what makes them similar or different to each other. Ask children a range of questions such as: How many groups can you make? Which characteristics did you look at most closely and why?

Have fun playing a whole-class game of 'Guess who?' whereby you choose a member of the class but do not reveal their identity. Children ask a range of yes/no questions based upon observable characteristics, such as: Have they got brown hair? Are they wearing grey socks?, and then eliminate class members who do not fit that description. The aim of the game is for children to correctly identify the person you have secretly chosen.

- **Asking relevant questions and using different types of science enquiries to answer them**
- **Making systematic and careful observations**

Animal classification

Children could begin by writing the names of a wide variety of animals onto individual Lego™ blocks (or onto a strip of masking tape stuck onto the side of each block) and then sort and classify these into fish, amphibians, reptiles, birds and mammals. They should use the blocks from each 'animal group' to build a tower and compare which tower contains the greatest variety of types and species. Throughout this topic, children should keep adding blocks to their towers each time they think of another animal and can identify the group to which it belongs.

Working scientifically

- **Gathering, recording, classifying and presenting data in a variety of ways to help in answering questions**
- **Recognise when and how secondary sources might help them to answer questions that cannot be answered through practical investigations (non-statutory notes and guidance)**

Statutory Requirement: explore and use classification keys to help group, identify and name a variety of living things in their local and wider environment.

Whole-class key

This activity works best outside in the playground. Ask children to suggest a way of dividing the whole group into two categories or sub groups. They will need to think of a question that can only be answered with either yes or no, such as 'Are you a boy?'. The agreed question could be written on the ground using chalk and then two arrows drawn facing outwards in different directions (one arrow for 'yes' and one arrow for 'no'). Every child should answer this question and follow the relevant arrow to stand in a new place. Continue with the process of writing questions and asking children to group themselves according to their responses until every child stands alone with their own mini whiteboard with their name written on.

Place the named whiteboards on the playground floor in these final positions and ask all children to form a large, mixed up group again. Imagine that individual children in the class are newly discovered species found during a recent expedition. Demonstrate how we can look at observable characteristics and use our giant key to group, identify and name unknown things easily.

Using and developing keys

A carousel of 'key activities' for children to move around can be great fun. Teams could use a key to identify 'My Little Pony' or 'Marvel Superhero' characters, premier league footballers or pop group members as well as devise their own keys for other groups to use.

Out and about

Ensure plenty of opportunities for children to use pre-prepared keys in the local and wider environment. An adventure around the school grounds or trip to a park, woodland or sea shore would allow children to use keys to identify and name unknown plants including flowers and trees as well as animals such as minibeasts and birds.

> Working scientifically
> - **Recording data and results of increasing complexity using scientific diagrams and labels, classification keys, tables, scatter graphs, bar and line graphs**
> - **They should use and develop keys and other information records to identify, classify and describe living things (non-statutory notes and guidance)**

Statutory Requirement: recognise that environments can change and that this can sometimes pose dangers to living things.

There are some inspiring children's books that can be used as a context for teaching about environmental changes. A favourite of mine is *The Lorax* by Dr. Seuss in which children can learn about the repercussions of cutting down the Truffula trees, which are the producers in the food chain, and the impact this has upon many other living things.

Research it

Children could work in 'expert' groups and use secondary sources to research how a number of endangered animals are being affected by environmental changes. Examples to include (as well as ideas suggested by children) could be:

- Water vole: the most endangered mammal species in the UK largely due to habitat loss through riverside and countryside development and also water pollution.
- Great Crested Newt: one of the most heavily protected species in the UK largely due to loss of ponds through farming and housing developments.

- Bee: rapid population decline thought to be partly due to farmers spraying their crops with insecticide and pesticide which are killing bees.

- Orangutan/panda/tiger: decline in populations of these well known animals in the wider environment are largely due to deforestation and the destruction of their habitats.

- Hammerhead shark: decline in populations due to these sharks mistaking plastic bags littering the oceans for food, such as jelly fish, which is killing them slowly.

There are excellent links with the lower Key Stage 2 English curriculum whereby children draft and rewrite persuasive articles and letters to a local newspaper, council, or large organisation such as the World Wildlife Fund in order to highlight the plight of their chosen animal and inform the public about conservation and protection.

Working scientifically

- **Reporting on findings from enquiries, including oral and written explanations, displays or presentations of results and conclusions**

- **Using straightforward scientific evidence to answer questions or to support their findings**

- **Recognise when and how secondary sources might help them to answer questions that cannot be answered through practical investigations (non-statutory notes and guidance)**

Living Things and their Habitats in Year 5

Before describing the life cycles of different animal groups, children could engage in a number of creative revision activities to ensure that they have a good understanding of what it means to be a mammal, amphibian, insect and bird.

Physical sorting

Secure a label or sticker onto the back of every child so that they cannot see which animal they are. Labels to include could be:

- mammals: dog, whale, human, kangaroo, leopard, mouse, rabbit, gorilla, hedgehog
- amphibians: frog, toad, newt, salamander
- insects: beetle, butterfly, moth, wasp, ant, ladybird, bee
- birds: owl, flamingo, ostrich, emu, eagle, robin, swan, goose, blackbird, peacock, penguin

Children should move around the room, asking their fellow classmates 'yes/no' questions in order to identify which animal they are. Questions such as: Do I have a tail? Would you find me in a zoo?

Can I fly? Do I have four legs? should be encouraged. Once every child knows which animal they are, they could play a game of 'corners' by listening carefully to a number of statements (covering content from previous programmes of study) and then grouping themselves accordingly. Statements might include:

- I am nocturnal/I am not nocturnal (diurnal)
- I am a predator/I am not a predator (prey)
- I am a carnivore/I am an omnivore/I am herbivore
- I am a mammal/I am an amphibian/I am an insect/I am a bird

After the physical sorting activity, children should work together in their final mammal, amphibian, insect and bird teams to produce a definition of what it means to be part of that group. A creative strategy is to use the words 'can, have, are' to prompt children's thinking, for example: mammals can produce milk, mammals have hair on their bodies and mammals are warm blooded.

Working scientifically

- **Raise different kinds of questions (non-statutory notes and guidance)**
- **Recording data and results of increasing complexity**

Statutory Requirement: describe the differences in the life cycles of a mammal, an amphibian, an insect and a bird.

Observation over time

There are some fantastic opportunities for children to care for and observe the hatching of chicks, tadpoles, butterflies, moths and even worms in the school environment. An internet search will soon put you in touch with innovative companies that offer a wealth of wonderful first-hand experiences and these should extend activities carried out in the Year 2 'Animals including Humans' topic described on page 23. The recording of children's observations made over a period of time can be done creatively through flip books, zig zag books, scrap books, diary entries, photo albums and time-lapse photography including PowerPoint presentations set to a very short slide transition.

Working scientifically

- **Make their own decisions about what observations to make (non-statutory notes and guidance)**
- **Recording data and results of increasing complexity using scientific diagrams and labels, classification keys, tables, scatter graphs, bar and line graphs**

Research it

Children could form expert teams according to the animal label they were given in the original sorting activities. They should research the life cycles of their animals using secondary sources such as the internet (there are some incredible life cycle video clips to be found) or by preparing questions for a knowledgeable visitor in school, a trip to the local library or an arranged library loan box on the topic of life cycles. Children should then pool their expertise in order to plan and present information gathered to the rest of the class.

This activity should culminate in children being able to identify the differences in life cycles between groups, as the statutory objective requires them to.

> Working scientifically
>
> - **Recording data and results of increasing complexity using scientific diagrams and labels, classification keys, tables, scatter graphs, bar and line graphs**
> - **Reporting and presenting findings from enquiries, including conclusions, causal relationships and explanations of and degree of trust in results, in oral and written forms such as display and other presentations**
> - **Recognise which secondary sources will be most useful to research their ideas and begin to separate opinion from fact (non-statutory notes and guidance)**

Statutory Requirement: describe the life process of reproduction in some plants and animals.

Plant reproduction

Children will have explored the part that flowers play in the life cycle of flowering plants during the Year 3 'Plants' topic (see page 11) and should recollect that sexual reproduction in flowering plants works by pollination, seed formation and seed dispersal. In Year 5, they should also learn that new plants can be created from just one plant (asexual reproduction). The non-statutory notes and guidance for this objective suggest that children *'might try to grow new plants from different parts of the parent plant, for example, seeds, stem and root cuttings, tubers, bulbs.'* The activities described below offer a few suggestions for how children might go about exploring this.

Can I use seeds from a plant to grow a new plant?

Children will enjoy the challenge of collecting seeds from vegetables such as peppers and pumpkins or fruit such as apples, tomatoes and watermelons and then washing them thoroughly before planting these in an attempt to grow a new plant. They should realise that the seeds might grow, but not always (they will have more success with seeds purchased from a nursery or garden centre), however it will be interesting to try and also revisit what plants need in order to grow from topics covered in previous years.

Re-growing vegetables from 'tops'

A fascinating activity for children is for them to cut the top off a carrot and place this in a saucer of water on a sunny window spot. Alternatively, they could place the 'stub' from celery or a lettuce (such as romaine lettuce) or the bottom end from spring onions upright in a shallow dish of water. They should change the water every few days and observe how the plants will sprout new foliage and continue to thrive.

An important aspect of working scientifically in upper Key Stage 2 is for children to be able to use test results to make predictions to set up further comparative and fair tests. They should, therefore, have opportunities to investigate what other plants they can re-grow in this way, record their findings and look for differences in growth rates.

Growing new plants from cuttings

Using a cutting from the non-flowering shoot of a plant (such as a fuchsia, begonia, coleus, geranium, ivy or mint), carefully remove the leaves from the bottom half of the stem and then use the remaining leaves to balance the cutting in a jam jar filled almost to the top with cold water. Change the water every two to three days and observe how the cuttings will soon produce a root system. When there are lots of roots, the cutting can be potted in compost and will continue to grow. Children should have opportunities to investigate with cuttings from different plants and use different growing mediums to find out which work best.

> Working scientifically
> - **Planning different types of scientific enquiries to answer questions, including recognising and controlling variables where necessary**
> - **Taking measurements, using a range of scientific equipment, with increasing accuracy and precision, taking repeat readings when appropriate**
> - **Recording data and results of increasing complexity using scientific diagrams and labels, classification keys, tables, scatter graphs, bar and line graphs**
> - **Using test results to make predictions to set up further comparative and fair tests**
> - **Reporting and presenting findings from enquiries, including conclusions, causal relationships and explanations of and degree of trust in results, in oral and written forms such as displays and other presentations**

Reproduction in animals

This area of learning should be linked to work covered earlier in the Year 2 'Animals including Humans' topic (see page 23) whereby children notice that animals have offspring which grow into adults. In

Year 5, children will learn that almost every animal uses sexual reproduction (male and female combined) to create offspring. They should be encouraged to research and compare how different animals reproduce and grow by asking and answering questions such as:

- Do all animals either give birth to live young or lay eggs?
- Why do some animals lay more eggs than they need?
- Can any male animals have babies?
- How do interesting animals such as seahorses, sharks, stick insects or fresh water turtles produce babies?
- Are all animals pregnant for the same amount of time? What can you find out about the gestation periods of different animals?

Note: Children will continue to learn about reproduction in living things during the Year 6 'Evolution and Inheritance' topic (see page 67) whereby they recognise that living things produce offspring of the same kind but normally offspring vary and are not identical to their parents.

Working scientifically

- **Reporting and presenting findings from enquiries, including conclusions, causal relationships and explanations of and degree of trust in results, in oral and written forms such as displays and other presentations**
- **Recognise which secondary sources will be most useful to research their ideas and begin to separate opinion from fact (non-statutory notes and guidance)**

Living Things and their Habitats in Year 6

Statutory Requirement: describe how living things are classified into broad groups according to common observable characteristics and based on similarities and differences, including micro-organisms, plants and animals.

Classification using observable characteristics

Recap from the Year 4 programme of study (described on page 48) that everything in the world can be classified into one of two very broad groups: living and non-living. Model this by using a globe to represent the world and then laying two lolly sticks facing outwards from the globe: label one stick 'living things' and the other 'non-living things'.

Explain that we are going to think more about the group of 'living things' and ask children how we might divide this into sub groups and what these might be. Take a number of suggestions before laying two more lolly sticks so that they branch outwards from 'living things' and label one 'plants' and the other 'animals'.

Note: There are other sub divisions to be made here (such as microorganisms) and these can be discussed with children and included in subsequent activities.

Challenge small groups of children to discuss and share ideas about how they would further subdivide and name the groups of 'plants' and then 'animals' based on similarities and differences. It is important to reassure there are no right or wrong answers at this point and that many scientists over the years have attempted to classify living things into groups with differing results.

Children should report on how and why they have grouped in their chosen ways, taking photographs as evidence of their classification ideas. They could learn about the Swedish biologist, Carl Linnaeus (1707–1778), who invented the classification system we use today by looking at observable characteristics including number of body parts, size, shape and methods of getting food.

A very simple version of his system, for this activity, might look like this:

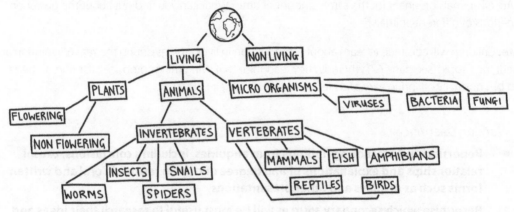

Working scientifically

- **Recording data and results of increasing complexity using scientific diagrams and labels, classification keys, tables, scatter graphs, bar and line graphs**

Classifying micro-organisms

Children could develop their skills of working scientifically and learn more about the broad group of microscopic living things we called micro-organisms. They could plan and carry out a number of activities to investigate fungi, such as finding out how to prevent mould growing on different types of bread or the conditions required for yeast to grow best.

Working scientifically

- **Planning different types of scientific enquiries to answer questions, including recognising and controlling variables where necessary**
- **Taking measurements, using a range of scientific equipment, with increasing accuracy and precision, taking repeat readings when appropriate**
- **Recording data and results of increasing complexity using scientific diagrams and labels, classification keys, tables, scatter graphs, bar and line graphs**
- **Using test results to make predictions to set up further comparative and fair tests**

- **Reporting and presenting findings from enquiries, including conclusions, causal relationships and explanations of and degree of trust in results, in oral and written forms such as displays and other presentations**

Articulate through art

Examining images of different micro-organisms, as they would look under the microscope, is a great way to find out more about them. Many striking examples of this can be found using a quick internet image search. Common viruses to include could be chickenpox, influenza, measles and mumps. In addition to this, bacteria to include could be food poisoning, pneumonia, soil bacteria and bacteria found in food such as yoghurt or cheese. Linking science with art, children could recreate these fascinating images using sketching, painting, printing and collage. They could also use secondary sources of information to find out more about both useful and harmful micro-organisms.

Ensure that children have opportunities to add the label 'micro-organisms' to the lolly stick classification activity described at the start of this topic and also name some of the different types they have been learning about, such as virus, bacteria and fungi.

Working scientifically

- **Recording data and results of increasing complexity using scientific diagrams and labels, classification keys, tables, scatter graphs, bar and line graphs**
- **Recognise which secondary sources will be most useful to research their ideas and begin to separate opinion from fact (non-statutory notes and guidance)**

Statutory Requirement: give reasons for classifying plants and animals based on specific characteristics.

I'll never remember that!

Children should look carefully at the common observable characteristics of a common plant and suggest a number of words to describe its appearance in detail. For example, a common daffodil could be described as having six yellow outer petals surrounding a trumpet shaped frilly cup, a tall green stem and long, thin, upwards-pointing leaves. They could try translating their descriptions into Latin using a translation website to put forwards possibilities of what this might have been named in the late 1700s.

Lots of fun can be had trying this activity for a range of common plants and animals before suggesting what the benefits and problems would have been with naming plants and animals in such a long and detailed way.

Working scientifically

- **Recognise which secondary sources will be most useful to research their ideas and begin to separate opinion from fact (non-statutory notes and guidance)**
- **Identifying scientific evidence that has been used to support or refute ideas or arguments**

Carl Linnaeus and a much easier system of naming

Linking science and English, children could research and write about the life and work of Swedish biologist Carl Linnaeus, who devised a new system of naming by giving each living thing just two Latin names. The first name identifies the group (or genus) to which it belongs and the second name tells you which type (or species) it is within that group, for example:

Dog-rose: *Rosa canina,* Mountain rose: *Rosa woodsii,* Field rose: *Rosa arvensis*

Tiger: *Panthera tigris,* Lion: *Panthera leo,* Jaguar: *Panthera onca,* Leopard: *Panthera pardus*

Note: This 'binomial' (two part) naming system is written in italics and the first word always starts with a capital letter.

A creative activity which encourages children to classify plants and animals based on specific characteristics is to challenge them to suggest names for newly discovered species using Linnaeus' two-part system. Pairs working together could give each of the examples below a common name and binomial Latin name and be able to explain how they have created these based on specific characteristics:

1 This new species of small fish is found in most tropical oceans around the world. It has a distinct red colour on the tips of its fins which looks like red nail varnish!

2 This new species of spider looks like it is doing cart-wheels as it spins itself away from predators.

3 This new species of flower is the only one known to open its petals at night and close them during the day.

Working scientifically

- **Reporting and presenting findings from enquiries, including conclusions, causal relationships and explanations of and degree of trust in results, in oral and written forms such as displays and other presentations**

- **Identifying scientific evidence that has been used to support or refute ideas or arguments**

4
A Creative Approach to Teaching Seasonal Changes

Seasonal changes in Year 1

Year 1 teachers should be creative with their planning for this topic and ensure that there are exciting opportunities throughout the year for children to get outside and explore the changing seasons, if possible every month or half term. My recommendation is to 'adopt' a tree in the school grounds or local environment so that children can make detailed observations of how it changes across the months and then record this through photographs, sketching and painting as well as note taking and spoken word.

Children might like to hear about American photographer, Mark Hirsch, who in 2012 purchased his first iPhone and, whilst learning how to use the camera, decided to take a photograph of his favourite tree every day for an entire year. His documentation of seasonal change is now published in a book entitled *That Tree*. Children could create a permanent display in the corner of their classroom of a tree that they can adapt to reflect the observations they have made.

Seize every opportunity possible to get outdoors and observe the changing seasons first-hand. Children could collect and create an autumn, winter, spring and summer seasonal tray or indoor garden whereby they can display seasonal items found in nature including changing leaves, buds, seeds, fruits and blooms for others to observe, explore and identify. They could record observations and measurements in a class big book entitled 'Our school through the year' and keep adding to this during seasonal activities. The book is a wonderful way for children to consolidate their learning as well as display as a celebration item to share with parents and visitors too.

There are some fantastic opportunities to link with the programme of study for art when recording observations over periods of time in a creative way. Techniques such as colour mixing, printing, weaving, rubbing, collage and photography are all appropriate ways for children to consolidate their understanding of the changing seasons.

Observing and describing weather associated with the seasons provides ample opportunities to link with the mathematics curriculum. Children can use a range of equipment to measure temperature, rainfall, wind speed and direction as well as record this information using simple charts, tables and graphs and look for patterns in data. Children will love scripting, presenting and filming their own weather reports using the data they have collected and there are strong links here to the statutory requirements of spoken language as described in the Key Stage 1 programme of study for English.

> **Statutory Requirement:** observe changes across the four seasons.
> **Statutory Requirement:** observe and describe weather associated with the seasons and how day length varies.

Activities for autumn

Welly walks and scavenger hunts

Get out and about for a 'Signs of autumn' hunt. Children could have pre-prepared pictorial spotter sheets to help them focus on what to look out for. This might include: conkers, damsons, garden spiders, dew drops on webs and grass, crunchy and coloured leaves, winged seeds, acorns, pinecones, bramble blackberries and fungi such as mushrooms. Another way to organise this is to give pairs of children a long egg box with at least ten compartments to fill with different autumnal items found on a hunt.

Playing autumn colour bingo is a fun activity whereby children have to find and identify a specified number of autumnal coloured items. Autumn leaf hunts link well to the Year 1 'Plants' unit described on page 5. Children can use simple identification picture cards or charts to name the leaves and trees as well as engage in a range of sorting, grouping and data handling activities.

Working scientifically

- **Observing closely, using simple equipment**
- **Identifying and classifying**

Investigating why some leaves change colour in the autumn

Explore first by drawing small circles onto filter paper and colouring them in with a good selection of felt tip pens. Drip a few drops of water onto each one and observe how some unexpected colours in the inks spread across the paper. It is important for young children to understand that these other colours have been there all the time but we don't see them because they are hidden by the main colour of the pen.

Now try a similar activity, but with real leaves: collect some green leaves, break or cut them into tiny pieces and put them into an empty jam jar or clear cup. Ask an adult to pour surgical spirit into the jar so that the leaves are just covered then mash and stir the leaves thoroughly until the liquid turns slightly green. Cover the jar loosely with cling film and place it carefully into a dish containing around 3 cm hot water.

Leave for up to an hour and then cut a clean strip of filter paper and dip one end into the liquid. The liquid will travel up the filter paper and, slowly, the colours from the leaves will separate out. Just like how the ink in the pens can be made up of different colours, the same goes for green leaves. In the autumn when there is less sunlight and some leaves lose their green colour, we see the other colours that have been there all year just waiting to be seen!

Note: Spinach leaves work particularly well for this activity.

Working scientifically

- **Observing closely, using simple equipment**
- **Performing simple tests**

- **Identifying and classifying**
- **Using their observations and ideas to suggest answers to questions**
- **Gathering and recording data to help in answering questions**

Weather forecasting with pine cones

Children could use a hand lens to observe the appearance of pine cones they have collected. They should notice that cones are usually open and learn about how this enables the seeds inside to be dispersed by the wind. They should compare the open cone to what happens when they hold one under water for several minutes – the cone will slowly close up to prevent the seeds from becoming damp and travelling only a short distance during dispersal. Children could secure a number of pine cones on a window sill outside and use this simple rule each day to help predict the weather: Is it going to rain today? Is it going to be dry today? Children could compare this to the actual predicted forecast in a television report, newspaper or on the internet.

Working scientifically
- **Asking simple questions and recognising that they can be answered in different ways**
- **Observing closely, using simple equipment**
- **Using their observations and ideas to suggest answers to questions**
- **Gathering and recording data to help in answering questions**

Activities for winter

Wrap up warm and get out in the local environment looking for signs of winter. A simple pictorial spotter sheet for winter could include items in nature such as an evergreen needle, a tree with no leaves, a leaf still on a tree, a prickly leaf, animal tracks in mud or snow, berries on branches, frost on plants or spider webs, icicles, snow, feathers and pinecones.

Evergreen and deciduous: an investigation

As a result of leaves falling during autumn, children will observe that many of the trees around them in the winter are now almost or completely bare. They will learn in the Year 1 'Plants' topic (see page 5) that a deciduous tree loses its leaves once a year as they dry out and fall off whereas an evergreen keeps its leaves all year long.

As an opportunity to work scientifically and investigate this further, groups of children could model different leaves by soaking three paper towels in a tray of water and then make observations over time of how quickly they dry out when hung outside on a washing line 'tree branch'. They should open one wet paper towel out flat to represent a broad deciduous leaf such as a sycamore, roll another wet paper towel up tightly to represent an evergreen needle, and fold the third wet paper towel in half between wax paper and secured with a giant paper clip to represent the waxy surface of an evergreen holly leaf.

Children could predict which 'leaves' they think might dry quickly or slowly and explain why they think this. After at least 30 minutes, they should discuss their observations and relate these to real examples of the leaves being represented and their chances of survival during cold, dry winter months.

They should share their ideas about how some leaves have a special protection, such as the waxy holly leaf and thin pine needle, and this enables them to keep their leaves all year round.

Working scientifically

- **Observing closely, using simple equipment**
- **Performing simple tests**
- **Identifying and classifying**
- **Using their observations and ideas to suggest answers to questions**
- **Gathering and recording data to help in answering questions**

How windy is it?

The UK is one of the windiest countries in Europe, with January reported to be the windiest month on average for the UK. Look for simplified versions of the Beaufort wind scale so that young children can make their own observations and use this to classify wind speeds on land. They can also measure wind speed by timing how long bubbles take to travel from one end of the playground to the other. Challenge individuals to race the bubbles and see if they can run faster than the wind!

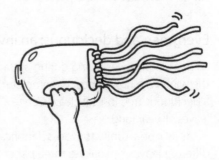

Make windsocks using unwanted socks, the sleeve from an old shirt or the top section of a milk carton with ribbons or strips of crêpe paper attached to the edge for children to use outside and observe wind direction. There are creative links to Key Stage 1 geography and mathematics objectives such as knowing about compass points and being able to describe position, direction and movement.

Working scientifically

- **Observing closely, using simple equipment**
- **Identifying and classifying**

- **Using their observations and ideas to suggest answers to questions**
- **Gathering and recording data to help in answering questions**

Changing clocks (1)

Around the end of October, children should observe how the mornings and evenings are gradually getting darker and the days are getting shorter. Children should be encouraged to discuss whether or not it was dark when they came home from school, when they had their evening meal or went to bed as well as observe and record the time on a morning when it begins to get light. It is interesting for children to know that the shortest daylight hours in the UK are on 21 December every year when the sun rises around 8 am and sets around 4 pm.

There are great reinforcement links here to the Year 1 mathematics curriculum whereby children begin to tell the time to the hour and half past the hour and draw the hands on a clock face to show these times.

Working scientifically
- **Using their observations and ideas to suggest answers to questions**
- **Gathering and recording data to help in answering questions**

Predicting and measuring temperature (1)

Winter is a perfect time to measure and record falling temperatures and look for patterns in data. Children should learn to use a range of thermometers including simple strip thermometers, window and wall thermometers (giant ones can be used for the whole class) and digital thermometers.

Children will have fun predicting the temperature every morning and then finding out how close they are with their guesses – it won't take long to improve their accuracy over just a few days! The winter time also enables us to learn about freezing temperatures and that temperature can even be colder than zero degrees Celsius!

Working scientifically
- **Observing closely, using simple equipment**
- **Gathering and recording data to help in answering questions**

Investigating snow

Whenever the opportunity arises, children will delight in being able to handle real snow and ice and investigate their properties. They could observe puddles outside freezing over or what happens when they sprinkle rock salt onto a frozen path as well as the melted remains of snowmen they have made. If the winter season does not bring snowfall then 'instant snow' can be bought cheaply in shops or from the internet. Children should add a small scoop of this white powder to water and make careful observations as it expands up to 100 times its original volume to look and feel like real snow.

Children could also make their own frozen figures or shapes by filling rubber gloves, balloons or jelly moulds with water and leaving these overnight in a freezer. Practical activities where they investigate how to delay or speed up melting provide excellent opportunities for children to work scientifically and experiment first-hand.

Working scientifically

- **Asking simple questions and recognising that they can be answered in different ways**
- **Observing closely, using simple equipment**
- **Using their observations and ideas to suggest answers to questions**

Activities for spring

March, April and May are my favourite months to take children hunting around the school grounds and local environment looking for signs of spring. Seasonal pictorial spotter sheets could include items in nature such as blossom, frogspawn, butterflies, caterpillars, catkins, birds and birds' nests, spring flowers such as the snowdrop, daffodil, primrose and crocus, buds appearing on branches and shoots appearing through soil.

Children could make a journey stick or a spring time bracelet using a strip of card with double sided sticky tape to peel back and secure interesting items they have collected along the way. This also makes a great memory prompt so that children can talk about what they identified and named during the activity. Another creative way to record signs of spring is to arrange four twigs or branches as a square or rectangle 'nature picture frame'. Children will need help to tie the corners in place with string and then add a 'glass' to the frame with a single piece of sticky back plastic. They can then simply secure the items they have collected to the sticky side of the adhesive roll and display this as a seasonal work of art.

Working scientifically

- **Observing closely, using simple equipment**
- **Identifying and classifying**
- **Gathering and recording data to help in answering questions**

Measuring rainfall

The season of spring is a great time of year to make accurate measurements of rainfall due to its sudden showers. Children could design and make their own rain gauge by cutting the top off a large pop bottle and placing this inverted into the remaining bottle so that it acts like a funnel to catch and collect rain water. This is a great opportunity for children to draw scales on sticks or wooden spoons and use these to measure capacity.

Recording data and looking at patterns in rainfall is a skill for children of this young age and can be done through them producing a 'real-life bar chart' by lining up tall measuring cylinders filled with water equivalent to the amount of rain fallen each week or even each month throughout the year. Learning about rainfall could also link to children testing waterproof materials for an umbrella or raincoat during the Year 1 'Materials' topic described on page 75.

Working scientifically

- **Observing closely, using simple equipment**
- **Gathering and recording data to help in answering questions**

Changing clocks (2)

After the cold, dark winter, children should begin to observe how the mornings and evenings are gradually getting lighter as the days are getting longer. They should discuss whether or not it was light when they woke up as well as observe and record the time on an evening when it begins to get dark. As with the 'Changing clocks (1)' activity described on page 63, there are cross curricular links to telling the time in the Year 1 mathematics curriculum. Children will be interested to learn that the longest daylight hours in the UK are on 21 June each year when the sun rises just before 5 am and sets just after 9 pm.

Working scientifically

- **Using their observations and ideas to suggest answers to questions**
- **Gathering and recording data to help in answering questions**

Activities for summer

Don your caps, T-shirts and sun cream and head out on a 'signs of summer' scavenger hunt. Items to include in this seasonal spotter sheet could be: large green leaves, flowers in full bloom such as daisy, dandelion, rose, red clover and honeysuckle, cleavers (stickyweed), bees visiting flowers, butterflies, birds feeding baby birds in nests, ladybirds, worms, rabbits and even hedgehogs. Playing summer colour bingo is a fun activity whereby children find and identify a specified number of bright and vivid coloured items that might be red, pink, green, purple, yellow, orange and blue.

Working scientifically

- **Observing closely, using simple equipment**
- **Identifying and classifying**

Sunshine and temperature

July is usually the hottest month in the UK with the most daily sunshine hours and an average temperature of around 19°C. Children will need to learn about sun safety and how to look after themselves in the higher temperatures. They could thread colour changing UV beads (which can be bought cheaply from the internet) onto pipe cleaners or thread to make bracelets and observe how they change to a dark colour when exposed to ultra violet rays in sunlight. The bracelets serve as a reminder for children to wear sun cream and also as a motivational context for them to ask their own questions about sunshine and high temperatures in summer.

Sunshine related activities will lay the foundations for later work in the Year 3 'Light' topic whereby children recognise that light from the sun can be dangerous and that there are ways to protect their eyes (see activities described on page 109).

Working scientifically

- **Asking simple questions and recognising that they can be answered in different ways**
- **Observing closely, using simple equipment**
- **Using their observations and ideas to suggest answers to questions**

Predicting and measuring temperature (2)

Summer is a perfect time to measure and record rising temperatures and look for patterns in data by creating simple pictograms and bar charts. Children should continue to use a range of thermometers including simple strip thermometers, window and giant wall thermometers as well as digital thermometers.

They will have fun predicting the temperature throughout the day and comparing how close they are with their guesses. They could also find out answers to questions such as: What is the highest temperature recorded for summer? How many days has it been since it rained? What was the coldest day in June and July?

Working scientifically

- **Observing closely, using simple equipment**
- **Gathering and recording data to help in answering questions**

5
A Creative Approach to Teaching Evolution and Inheritance

Although the title of this topic appears only once in the primary science curriculum, children will have already learnt about human life cycles and reproduction in both Year 2 'Animals including Humans' (see page 23) and Year 5 'Living Things and their Habitats' topics (see pages 51). A simple introduction to how fossils are formed is taught when children learn about 'Rocks' in Year 3 (described on page 101) and, finally, they will have identified that most living things live in habitats to which they are suited and that environments can change in the Year 2 and Year 4 'Living Things and their Habitats' topic (activities found on pages 43 and 48). Teachers of Year 6 should not be daunted by this topic (as many are), and simply embrace opportunities to extend prior learning in each of these areas.

Evolution and Inheritance in Year 6

> **Statutory Requirement:** recognise that living things have changed over time and that fossils provide information about living things that inhabited the Earth millions of years ago.

A fossil analogy

There are a number of creative ways to help children to understand what fossils are and how they provide us with useful information. One of my favourites is to take a single slice of white bread to represent the ocean floor and place a couple of jelly sweets, such as worms, shrimps or bears, onto this to represent dead organisms that have died and sunk to the bottom of the ocean. Now use slices of different types of bread, such as brown, wholemeal, granary and more white to represent layers of sediment collecting, settling and building up on top of each other over millions of years.

Add some heavy books on top of the stack to represent pressure on the layers which, over time, would cause the sediment to turn to hard rock. Leave for up to five days and observe how the bread has been compressed and now feels hard. Children could use a clear, broad milkshake straw to push down and 'drill' into the bread and take a 'rock' sample to observe the different layers of sediment that have built up over millions of years!

Children should try to separate the lower layers of 'rock' and examine the imprint made by the edible 'creatures' that were trapped long ago. Children can learn a lot about the size, shape and features of these organisms from the impression or fossil that has been created. It is important for children to understand that, over millions of years, the original organism would not remain as it would have rotted away or been eaten by predators, unlike the sweets which are still in their original solid form.

Fossil detectives

Gather together a selection of real fossils as well as intriguing images of different types of fossils – try to include a fossilised skull, eggs, teeth, footprints, skin, plants such as ferns, insects trapped in hardened tree sap, ammonites and even poo (coprolites)! Place these around the room and ask children to work as fossil detectives to try to identify what each one might have been and, more importantly, what we could learn from them, such as the diet, habitat, features and size of living things in the past.

Children could use secondary sources to research more recent fossil findings, such as hundreds of fossilised sauropod footprints discovered in Scotland and also fossilised hadrosaur bones found in Alaska both in 2015. There are creative links to the English curriculum whereby children could research and write biographical text about pioneering palaeontologist Mary Anning as well as newspaper headlines and reports heralding new and important discoveries.

Statutory Requirement: recognise that living things produce offspring of the same kind, but normally offspring vary and are not identical to their parents.

There are some fun and novel activities for introducing the concept that living things produce similar but not identical offspring to their parents (a quick internet search will point you in the right direction). Some examples include researching and discussing the family tree of fictional television characters such as The Simpsons, The Flintstones or the Addams Family. Children should look for similarities and differences between siblings in these unusual families and link this to inherited characteristics from parents.

Children could bring in photographs from home of mums, dads, siblings and other family members in order to identify and discuss inherited characteristics. Alternatively, they could examine images of famous celebrities such as current sports, film and music stars and then attempt to match these up with photographs printed from the internet of their lesser known siblings or parents, giving reasons for their choices.

- **Reporting and presenting findings from enquiries, including conclusions, causal relationships and explanations of and degree of trust in results, in oral and written forms such as displays and other presentations**
- **Identifying scientific evidence that has been used to support or refute ideas or arguments**

> **Statutory Requirement:** identify how animals and plants are adapted to suit their environment in different ways and that adaptation may lead to evolution.

Investigating animal adaptations (1)

During his famous voyage around the world, setting off from England in 1831, Charles Darwin visited the Galapagos Islands in the Pacific Ocean and observed that finches on different islands had gradually evolved different shaped beaks. He suggested that their beaks had adapted to the type of food that was available, otherwise they may have died out and become extinct.

Children could explore Darwin's ideas by using a range of utensils such as spoons, chopsticks, tweezers, tongs and pegs to represent different bird's beak shapes. They could investigate how many of different food types including string or pipe cleaners (worms), seeds (bird seed), rice (small insects), raisins (fruit and berries) and large marshmallows (meat and flesh) they can pick up with each 'bird beak' utensil in an agreed amount of time and record this information appropriately. Finally, children should form conclusions about the type of food most suited to different beak shapes and which types of birds would be more likely to be found in these environments.

Working scientifically

- **Recording data and results of increasing complexity using scientific diagrams and labels, classification keys, tables, scatter graphs, bar and line graphs**
- **Reporting and presenting findings from enquiries, including conclusions, causal relationships and explanations of and degree of trust in results, in oral and written forms such as displays and other presentations**
- **Identifying scientific evidence that has been used to support or refute ideas or arguments**

Investigating animal adaptations (2)

Before 1845, a population of peppered moths lived around the city of Manchester, England. They would camouflage themselves against the trunks of pale birch trees to avoid being eaten by birds and so it was the light grey variety of the moth that was most likely to survive and reproduce. However, around 1845, the city became more industrialized, and pollution slowly turned the bark of the trees to a darker grey colour. Now it was the dark grey moths that could hide from their predators and they became far more numerous than the pale variety.

In the mid-twentieth century, as air pollution was reduced and tree trunks became cleaner, the light grey moths became more common again.

As a practical example of this, scatter an equal number of short strands of white, grey and black wool (representing different varieties of Peppered moth) across a large piece of white fabric or paper (representing light coloured tree bark) and then ask children to act as birds and hunt for as many strands that they can find in 30 seconds. They should compare the total number of each colour collected (using tweezers to represent a bird's beak) and discuss why they think different coloured 'moths' had a different chance of survival. This activity could be repeated by scattering the same strands of wool across a large piece of black fabric or paper and any interesting results should be linked to the story of the Peppered moth, with a discussion of how adaptation may lead to evolution.

Working scientifically

- **Recording data and results of increasing complexity using scientific diagrams and labels, classification keys, tables, scatter graphs, bar and line graphs**
- **Using test results to make predictions to set up further comparative and fair tests**
- **Reporting and presenting findings from enquiries, including conclusions, causal relationships and explanations of and degree of trust in results, in oral and written forms such as displays and other presentations**
- **Identifying scientific evidence that has been used to support or refute ideas or arguments**

Investigating plant adaptations

There are some incredible plant adaptations for children to research and marvel at! A focus on how certain plants survive in a rainforest environment will highlight specific adaptations to tropical conditions such as lack of light, poor soils, protection from predators and heavy rainfall. Children could investigate how the shape of the leaf may or may not help it to dry quickly by dripping water (using a pipette to mimic rainfall) onto different leaf shapes.

Note: Real leaves or templates (see below) cut out from card, laminated or even waterproof paper can be used for this activity.

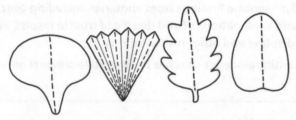

Groups working together should observe how easily the water drains away from each shape or how it stays on the leaf for an amount of time. Using their observations, children could design a 'super leaf' that has the best chance of surviving in the rainforest. They will need to think carefully about the shape their leaf has adapted and explain how this enables it to dry quickly after heavy rainfall and why this might be important.

Using secondary sources of information, children could find out more about plants such as the Fan Palm whose leaves are pleated and segmented or the Weeping Fig with its downward-pointing 'drip tip' – both of which are adapted to allow rapid removal of water from the leaf surface. Children might also investigate why some leaves have a waxy surface, by covering leaf templates with greaseproof or wax paper and comparing the time taken for 'rainfall' to drain away.

Working scientifically

- **Planning different types of scientific enquiries to answer questions, including recognising and controlling variables where necessary**
- **Taking measurements, using a range of scientific equipment, with increasing accuracy and precision, taking repeat readings when appropriate**
- **Recording data and results of increasing complexity using scientific diagrams and labels, classification keys, tables, scatter graphs, bar and line graphs**
- **Using test results to make predictions to set up further comparative and fair tests**
- **Reporting and presenting findings from enquiries, including conclusions, causal relationships and explanations of and degree of trust in results, in oral and written forms such as displays and other presentations**

Chemistry

6
A Creative Approach to Teaching Materials

Children should develop an awareness of how materials make up everything around us and can be found anywhere and everywhere. For example, if a young child in Year 1 held up an object he had found in the classroom and asked, 'Is this made out of a material?' he would hear a chorus of 'Yes of course ... everything is a material!'.

There are unusual and rare materials to be found in our world and these can fuel children's interest and curiosity, however, starting with the most common materials such as wood, plastic, glass, metal, fabric and rock and then including materials such as brick, paper, cardboard, elastic, foil, rubber and ceramic will lay an excellent foundational knowledge throughout the primary age range.

Everyday Materials in Year 1

> **Statutory Requirement:** distinguish between an object and the material from which it is made.
> **Statutory Requirement:** identify and name a variety of everyday materials, including wood, plastic, glass, metal, water and rock.

Starting with a huge bag of 'treasure' or recycling makes an intriguing opening activity to get the whole class thinking about both of the requirements described above. Involve children in rummaging for interesting items, naming, examining and exploring, discussing observable properties and then having a go at identifying the material from which each object is made. This kind of activity leads to a range of interesting sorting and grouping opportunities and is a key requirement for both working scientifically and mathematics at this age.

Santa's sorting

I have enjoyed teaching this activity in the winter months using the context of Santa's sack of toys that have either been broken, are undeliverable or unwanted. You could include items such as:

- wood – 'ball and cup' game, wooden cricket bat, wooden building block, wooden jigsaw piece, single drum stick

- plastic – plastic tea set with items missing or broken, golf ball, doll with an arm missing, bucket with handle missing, plastic spade, plastic water pistol, Lego™ blocks
- glass – glass marble, snow globe, glass eye from a teddy bear, magnifying glass, glass chess piece
- metal – cymbal with the handle missing, triangle with no beater, metal 'matchbox type' car, metal slinky, metal K'Nex™ or Meccano™ piece, nuts and bolts
- rock – stone paper weight, sticks of chalk, ceramic ornament
- rubber – bouncy ball, single wellington boot, rubber duck, squeezy dog toy or bath toy, eraser, single rubber glove, popped balloon, loom bands.

Children could be invited to sort and group the objects into piles of toys in a range of different ways before using the criteria of 'objects made from the same material'. They could write labels to name these groups of materials or distribute Santa's labels that have become mixed up.

Working scientifically
- **Observing closely**
- **Identifying and classifying**

Guessing games

Games such as 'What's in the box?' or 'Twenty questions' are brilliant for helping children to develop their questioning skills and ability to distinguish between an object and the material from which it is made. Each day, hide a different mystery object in a bag or box. Children ask questions such as: 'Is it see-through?', 'Is it found at school?', 'Is it smooth?', 'Can you break it easily?' until they are able to guess correctly what the mystery object is and also the material from which it is made. Examples of items to include in the box could be: a glass hand lens, a metal coin, a plastic spoon, a fabric cap, a paper aeroplane and so on.

Working scientifically
- **Asking simple questions**
- **Identifying and classifying**

Materials hunting

Every Year 1 class should go on a materials hunt around their classroom, school building, outdoors or at home. Organise the children into ability groups and give each team an identical envelope containing labels for: wood, plastic, glass, metal, fabric, rock, paper, cardboard, fabric, water and a few blank labels.

Organise the rota so that the lowest ability group hunts first and must answer the question: 'What can you find that is made from ...?' by sticking their labels onto the actual items and objects that they find. For example, they might stick the label 'plastic' onto a pencil pot or the label 'glass' onto a window until they have found an object for all of their labels. This activity gets trickier depending on where in the rota your group is. The highest ability children will have to hunt hard to find enough items unlabelled by the previous groups! By including blank labels you will allow all groups of children to look for additional materials rather than restricting the search to just those that have been discussed so far.

Note: Include 'water' in the labels for this activity as it is a material suggested in the statutory requirements for Year 1. It is important that children begin learning about this topic with an understanding that liquids are materials too.

Link materials hunts to books such as *We're Going on a Bear Hunt* by Michael Rosen. As a class, you can make suggestions for a new version of the story and think creatively about the words you could choose or invent to represent the properties of different materials, such as:

Uh oh! Glass – shiny, smooth, see-through glass ... clink, smash, clink, smash!

Uh oh! Paper – smooth, cool, scrunchy, paper ... swoosh, crunch, swoosh, crunch!

Working scientifically

● **Identifying and classifying**

● **Using their observations and ideas to suggest answers to questions**

Collecting materials

Each class could make a display of interesting items they have collected made from wood and then the following week, plastic and so on. This is a great way to challenge children to look around and identify objects made from everyday materials and to recognise that some of these might also be made from more than one material. Asking every child to find one example of each material also saves the teacher hunting around for a vast selection every week too!

Children should also recognise that there are different types of wood, plastic, metal and paper etc. Young children will be surprised to learn that foil is a type of metal, as they tend to think of it as a type of crinkly, shiny paper. Children can also be fascinated to learn the specific names of materials, such as polythene bag instead of plastic bag and aluminium can instead of metal can and also to distinguish between so many different types of fabric such as wool, fur, silk, cotton, polyester, leather and so on.

Display objects in their named material groups within a gigantic sorting circle made from string in the school hall or chalked out on the playground floor. Children can make labels for each category of material and, if possible, a photograph could be taken looking down (as a bird's eye view) for evidence of this exciting large scale activity.

Working scientifically

- **Observing closely**
- **Identifying and classifying**

Statutory Requirement: describe the simple physical properties of a variety of everyday materials.

Feely boards, walls, books, handprints and collages

Children should get 'hands-on' and experience for themselves the simple properties of everyday materials. Use real examples of a wide range of fabrics such as silk, lycra, cotton, voile, fur, suede, denim, netting as well as other wonderfully tactile materials such as bubble wrap, corrugated card, tissue paper, crêpe paper, foil, sponge – anything you can get your hands on really!

Open ended exploration encourages young children to use all of their senses and generate a whole-class collection of property words, such as: hard/soft; stretchy/stiff; shiny/dull; rough/smooth; bendy/not bendy ... as well as many, many others. There are opportunities here to learn more about how words can be related as opposites too. Children will also enjoy creating and using their own property words to describe different materials such as 'crinkly', 'scrunchy', 'crumply', 'tickly' and 'floaty'.

Creating feely boards, walls, books, handprints or collages are a great way for little hands to record simple properties of materials. 'Lift the flap' examples can be passed to other children to try to guess the property words being represented before looking under the material to reveal the answer.

Working scientifically

- **Observing closely**
- **Identifying and classifying**
- **Gathering and recording data to help in answering questions**

Statutory Requirement: compare and group together a variety of everyday materials on the basis of their simple physical properties.

This topic provides some fantastic opportunities for children to work scientifically. They should ask and answer questions about the properties of everyday materials by exploring for themselves and working practically with their peers. Choose from these simple, creative investigations for Year 1 children to carry out with support and guidance.

Waterproof/not waterproof

Challenge children to invent a new umbrella or design the roof for a house or shelter. Provide each group with pre-cut squares (around 15 cm x 15 cm) of a range of materials such as: sponge, plastic bag, foil, felt and cloth. They should work independently if possible by placing a square of material over the top of a transparent plastic cup and securing this with an elastic band. To represent rain falling, they could drip water, using a pipette, onto each material and make simple comparisons depending on the amount of water that has dripped through into each cup.

Some children might decide to place an item inside their cups, such as a toy figure or a cotton wool ball, so that they can see and feel how wet this has become. They should use this information to make and justify their choice of waterproof material as a solution to their original challenge.

See-through/not see-through (opaque/transparent)

The context of making a pair of curtains for a baby's bedroom or a sleep mask to wear on a long aeroplane flight provides the challenge for young children to carry out simple tests and find answers for themselves.

As in the waterproof example above, children can work independently by holding (or securing with an elastic band) pre-cut squares of a range of fabrics such as: denim, netting, cotton, dark coloured voile and leather over the lit end of a torch. They could shine the light towards a white wall or piece of card and compare how see-through (transparent) each material is. It is interesting for children to observe that black or dark materials are not always the best at blocking the light!

Stretchy/not stretchy

Children will have a lot of fun with this one, working safely in pairs to see how far they can stretch a range of materials (pre-cut into 30 cm strips) such as a woollen scarf, lycra leotard, cotton shirt, crepe paper, elastic hair bobble and nylon tights. There are creative opportunities for data handling whereby the class could make a giant bar chart using their stretched materials stapled down or lengths of string cut to represent the distances stretched.

> Working scientifically
> - **Asking simple questions and recognising that they can be answered in different ways**
> - **Observing closely, using simple equipment**
> - **Performing simple tests**

- **Identifying and classifying**
- **Using their observations and ideas to suggest answers to questions**
- **Gathering and recording data to help in answering questions**

Uses of Everyday Materials in Year 2

The Year 2 'Materials' topic should have some overlap with that from the previous year, therefore, teachers of both age groups should plan together to ensure that children have plenty of opportunities to develop progression in their conceptual understanding.

> **Statutory Requirement:** identify and compare the suitability of a variety of everyday materials, including wood, metal, plastic, glass, brick, rock, paper and cardboard for particular uses.

Materials munchers

An exciting recap of everyday materials involves children making their own 'materials munchers' using boxes and packaging with a pre-cut 'letter box' mouth through which to 'feed' a variety of items! The class could be organised into groups who must choose the most appropriate materials, from a mixed up assortment, to decorate their 'munchers'. Examples might include:

- metal muncher: aluminium foil, nuts, bolts, screws, coins, wire, paper clips, bottle tops, keys
- wood muncher: wooden lolly and cocktail sticks, twigs, tree bark, pegs and wooden spoons
- plastic muncher: plastic bags, cling film or bubble wrap, plastic cutlery, plastic packaging such as polystyrene egg cartons, Lego™ or Duplo™ blocks, CDs, sequins and bottle tops
- glass muncher: a tricky one to decorate safely in the classroom! Children could cut objects and items made from glass out of catalogues and magazines and use these to cover and decorate the box. They could also use glass beads to make facial features
- paper muncher: a wide range of paper types should be available in the primary school, such as writing, drawing, tissue, crêpe, news, tracing as well as items such as art straws and coloured sticky notes
- fabric muncher: samples including wool, fur, leather, suede, voile, netting, denim and cotton.

Children could sort a selection of real objects into groups according to which ones they would feed to each muncher, they could post a variety of 'everyday object' picture cards through the munchers' mouths according to what they would eat, they could make further suggestions for what else each one might munch on, they could recognise that some objects are made from more than one material and answer questions such as: Which muncher would munch on a spoon? Finally, they could design a new 'muncher' that munches on an additional material.

- **Identifying and classifying**
- **Using their observations and ideas to suggest answers to questions**

More materials hunting

Following on from a materials hunt in Year 1 (described on page 76), children should be encouraged to identify objects made from a wider range of materials such as wood, plastic, glass, metal, rock, paper, cardboard, brick, fabric, elastic, rubber, and ceramic. They could also be helped to discover and identify any unknown or unusual materials.

To ensure adequate progression from Year 1, children should answer questions relating to properties and uses of materials, such as: Why is the wall made of brick? Why is the window made of glass? Why is the gate made of metal? Why is the fence made of wood? Why is the sign made of plastic? Why is the ground made of concrete?

Similarly, children should be prompted to think about which materials have not been spotted on the hunt and suggest reasons as to why this might be the case: Why have we found nothing made of elastic? Where might we find this material?

Working scientifically

- **Observing closely, using simple equipment**
- **Identifying and classifying**
- **Using their observations and ideas to suggest answers to questions**

Ridiculous materials

Higher order thinking activities are a great way for children to consider the suitability of materials according to their properties. A popular example is to ask children to suggest the most ridiculous object that could be made out of a material and then explain why they think this and also what it should be made from. My favourite example of this was when I asked Year 2 children to suggest the most ridiculous object that could be made out of glass. The majority of children focused in on the fragile property of glass and how breakable it can be, suggesting mostly footballs and cricket bats, however, one girl suggested a secret diary due to the transparent property of glass and how unsuitable it would be for keeping the written contents a secret!

Riddles and rhymes

There are opportunities to link science with creative writing whereby children choose a material and identify its properties and uses in a descriptive verse, such as:

'I could be a bottle bobbing about in a fast, flowing stream. I could be a spoon mixing and stirring delicious, hot soup. I could be the last coloured block at the top of a toppling tower and I could be a frisbee whirling through the air on a sunny day in the busy park. Do you know what I am? I am plastic.'

- **Identifying and classifying**
- **Using their observations and ideas to suggest answers to questions**

More materials testing: who's afraid of the big bad wolf?

Many Key Stage 1 classes use the story of the Three Little Pigs as a motivating context for learning about the suitability of materials. Children will rise to the challenge of making model houses and shelters out of straw, wood (lolly sticks or twigs) and bricks (building blocks or play-based construction materials bought online such as Teifoc) as well as alternative everyday materials. Activities should culminate in children observing what happens in a range of simple tests including blowing the houses with a hairdryer which can easily be transformed into the big bad wolf using some fur and two large googly eyes!

Absorbent/not-absorbent

Alternative materials tests, which have not been carried out in Year 1, could include an absorbency investigation. A simple way of doing this is to drip water (coloured with a few drops of food colouring) using a pipette onto a range of everyday materials and observe how much of this is soaked into the material or how much can be squeezed back out into an empty, clear cup. Examples of materials to test could be: cotton wool, kitchen roll, cling film, aluminium foil, wax paper, sponge, polythene bag and newspaper.

Absorbency tests work well in the context of children finding a good material to make a baby's nappy or to mop up a spilt drink quickly; in these cases you could use weak orange or blackcurrant juice respectively in order to make these contexts more realistic.

Testing shock absorbency

Year 2 children could find out which materials protect a fragile object, such as an uncooked egg, when it is dropped from a height. Present a number of sealable bags filled with everyday materials such as: scrunched-up newspaper, cotton wool, expanded polystyrene packaging, sponge and even water. Place one egg amongst the material in each bag and ask children to suggest which they think will prevent the egg from breaking when it is dropped and explain why. Children's stories such as *Egg Drop* by Mini Grey and *Who Pushed Humpty Dumpty?* by David Levinthal and John Nickle provide a motivating context for this 'eggciting' test Children of all ages, are eager to inspect the contents of each bag after the 'drop' and compare what has actually happened with their original ideas.

- **Asking simple questions and recognising that they can be answered in different ways**
- **Observing closely, using simple equipment**
- **Performing simple tests**

- **Identifying and classifying**
- **Using their observations and ideas to suggest answers to questions**
- **Gathering and recording data to help in answering questions**

> **Statutory Requirement:** find out how the shapes of solid objects made from some materials can be changed by squashing, bending, twisting and stretching.

Although there are no 'official' physics topics in the Key Stage 1 science curriculum, this statutory objective enables children to learn about the ways in which some materials can change shape when simple forces are applied.

Move it

A creative introductory activity is to ask children to make body shapes or movements that represent a push, pull, squash, bend, twist and stretch. If they can move their own bodies in these ways, they can show their understanding of the terminology involved. There are links to the physical education curriculum whereby children can work together to share their ideas before adapting, improving and combining movements, and even performing their sequences as a simple composition set to music.

Make it

Children could work in small groups to squash, bend, twist and stretch lumps of play-dough into specified numbers, letters or shapes within a given time limit. They must be able to explain how they achieved the outcome of their sculpting, using the appropriate vocabulary for this objective.

Working scientifically
- **Using their (observations and) ideas to suggest answers to questions**
- **Gathering and recording data to help in answering questions**

Test it

In order to find out how the shapes of solid objects made from some materials can be changed by squashing, bending, twisting and stretching, children need to do exactly this. A selection of objects made out of everyday materials such as a pebble, sponge, deflated balloon, elastic hair bobble, tennis ball, pipe cleaner and ruler could be tested and children supported to record their observations in a simple printed table.

Working scientifically
- **Observing closely**
- **Performing simple tests**
- **Identifying and classifying**

- **Using their observations and ideas to suggest answers to questions**
- **Gathering and recording data to help in answering questions**

The curly wurly stretching world record

Children of any age love hearing about world record attempts and achievements. A particular favourite of mine is the squashing, bending, twisting and stretching of a popular chocolate bar and this makes an engaging context for learning about how the shapes of solid objects can be changed. The record stands, as this book goes to print, at a 26 g bar of Curly Wurly being stretched to an unbroken length of 311.5 cm in three minutes. Ask children to consider how this might have been achieved before giving each child a 26 g ball of play-dough and three minutes on the timer to change the shape of the dough into the longest length possible.

The rules of the world record state that once the material has been split or broken, you cannot fix it back together again and, therefore, children must work carefully to extend the shape without mishap. The activity provides creative opportunities to link science and mathematics whereby children measure and compare lengths using both non-standard and standard units.

Working scientifically
- **Observing closely, using simple equipment**
- **Using their observations and ideas to suggest answers to questions**
- **Gathering and recording data to help in answering questions**

Materials in Year 3

Although there is no officially named 'Materials' topic in the Year 3 programme of study for science, there are some superb activities for children to compare, group, indentify and investigate different kinds of rocks and soil in the 'Rocks' topic (described on page 99) as well as investigate reflective materials or which materials are best for making shadows, whilst learning about 'Light' (see page 107). Year 3 children will also compare how things move on different surfaces as well as identify, compare and group magnetic and non-magnetic materials during 'Forces and Magnets' activities (described on page 123). It seems that children will no doubt be 'materials experts' by the time they reach the end of Year 3!

States of Matter in Year 4

The most obvious unit for children to learn about materials in Year 4 is that entitled, 'States of Matter'. In addition to this, there are opportunities for testing, identifying, sorting and grouping materials that are conductors and insulators during the 'Electricity' topic (described on page 135).

Statutory Requirement: compare and group materials together, according to whether they are solids, liquids or gases.

Before children begin to compare and group materials according to whether they are solids, liquids or gases, it is vital that they have a secure understanding of what this actually means. Creative 'starter activities' are a great way of assessing prior knowledge as well as introducing or revisiting key vocabulary.

Ballooning around

Presenting sealed balloons containing ice (fill the balloon with water and leave in the freezer for a few days), water (fill the balloon with water) and air (simply blow the balloon up) for children to label and explore is a great way for them to start thinking about the simple properties of solids, liquids and gases. Groups working together should have their own balloons to handle and compare so that they can feel for themselves how solids can be hard, with a fixed shape whilst liquids and gases can feel 'squashy', with a changing shape. Children should also observe what happens when they cut and remove the outer skin of the balloons (over a small tray or bowl) and discuss how the solid keeps its shape, the liquid flows and takes the shape of the container whilst the gas spreads out to fill all the space available (although we can't actually see it).

Working scientifically

- **Making systematic and careful observations and, where appropriate, taking accurate measurements using standard units, using a range of equipment, including thermometers and data loggers**
- **Identifying differences, similarities or changes related to simple scientific ideas and processes**

Opportunities for children to talk about criteria for grouping, sorting and classifying are plentiful here and also link to elements of statistics in the mathematics curriculum such as using information presented in charts and pictograms. The activities are always more meaningful when real objects are used, so perhaps children could bring items in from home.

Shopping bag sorting

Ask groups of children to sort a range of well known items from a shopping bag, such as a bar of soap, plastic bowl, wooden spoon, bag of sugar, bottle of ketchup, can of fizzy drink, mouth wash, tube of toothpaste, can of shaving foam, sponge and bottle of perfume. To begin with, they should sort and group items however they wish to, using their own criteria such as colour, whether you would eat it or not, how heavy it feels etc. Do not prescribe to children how you want them to set this out; rather explain that equipment such as hoops, string or baskets could be made available if requested. Photographs of initial categories should be taken and used to compare the different ways in which sorting can be presented.

Working together and sharing their ideas, children should now attempt to sort the objects according to their state. The varying results will lead you to some enlightening pre-assessment evidence, whereby some children will have sorted the objects in a very distinct way, separating solids, liquids and gases. Other children's sorting may result in overlapping hoops to show how some solids can also be liquids (e.g. the bottle is plastic but the mouthwash is liquid) or some liquids can also be gas (e.g. the shaving foam is liquid in the can but contains air when it is squirted out). The most advanced thinkers might even have three hoops all overlapping – with a potential of seven categories! As long as children can justify their decisions then all suggestions should be acknowledged and discussed.

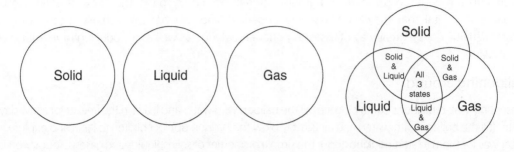

Sorting activities are a brilliant way of uncovering children's misconceptions about solids, liquids and gases so take lots of photographs as evidence! Quite often, solids such as sugar, salt and sand will be categorised as a liquid due to the fact that they flow and can be poured. Explain to children that a single grain of each of these substances will keep its shape and, therefore, is correctly defined as a solid. Toothpaste is a really confusing one to classify and, for children of this age, could be described as a mixture of solid and liquid or a solid with some liquid properties.

Working scientifically

- **Gathering, recording, classifying and presenting data in a variety of ways to help in answering questions**
- **Recording findings using simple scientific language, drawings, labelled diagrams, keys, bar charts and tables**
- **Talk about criteria for grouping, sorting and classifying (non-statutory notes and guidance)**

> **Statutory Requirement:** observe that some materials change state when they are heated or cooled, and measure or research the temperature at which this happens in degrees Celsius (°C).

Children should have lots of opportunities to explore and discuss everyday examples of materials changing state when they are either heated or cooled before advancing to more in-depth investigation. Real life situations ranging from snow melting on a path, ice melting on a car windscreen, chocolate melting in your hand, butter melting on toast, wax melting on a candle, ice-cream melting on a sunny day as well as puddles freezing in winter, or making your own ice pops, cubes and lollies will help them to link changing state with temperature.

Investigate it

Children will enjoy heating and cooling chocolate in order to make a range of tasty treats such as crispy cakes or chocolate buttons just as much as tasting the end products of an activity where they have made ice pops, lollies or 'slushies'.

Don't miss the opportunity to turn these activities into controlled investigations, for example: newly made chocolate crispy cakes from the same batch could be placed in different locations such as on top of a radiator, on a windowsill, on the teacher's desk, in a cupboard, under a table, outside, in a fridge and in a freezer. Groups working together should time how long it takes for their cakes to 'set' or solidify and then data collected can be compared and discussed.

Working scientifically

- **Asking relevant questions and using different types of scientific enquiries to answer them**
- **Setting up simple practical enquiries, comparative and fair tests**
- **Reporting on findings from enquiries, including oral and written explanations, displays or presentations of results and conclusions**
- **Using results to draw simple conclusions, make predictions for new values, suggest improvements and raise further questions**

Investigating melting and freezing points

Observing how materials change when they are heated and cooled enables children to carry out and record careful observations over time. Encourage them to put forward their own suggestions about how they could find out the melting and freezing points of different materials. There are some brilliant opportunities to link science with mathematics whereby children develop their understanding of temperature and measure accurately in standard units using thermometers and data loggers.

Melting point investigations are more easily carried out in the primary classroom using small amounts of materials such as wax, butter, pasta, ice, chocolate and cheese placed into foil cases and floated in large open bowls filled with different temperatures of water. Children can make careful observations of which materials begin to melt as well as take measurements of the temperature of the water when they see this happening. For less able children, liquid crystal thermometers (0–75°C) are waterproof strips that float on the surface of the water and change colour depending on how hot or cold it is.

Alternatively, the materials in their foil cases could be placed on sealed hot water bottles containing different temperatures of water. Another successful way of doing this is to seal small samples of individual materials in strong transparent plastic bags and immerse them in jugs containing different temperatures of water. Again, liquid crystal strip thermometers work brilliantly stuck onto the side of hot water bottles, cups and jugs for a safe and practical way to measure temperature.

Working scientifically

- **Setting up simple practical enquiries, comparative and fair tests**
- **Making systematic and careful observations and, where appropriate, taking accurate measurements using standard units, using a range of equipment, including thermometers and data loggers**
- **Reporting on findings from enquiries, including oral and written explanations, displays or presentations of results and conclusions**
- **Identifying differences, similarities or changes related to simple scientific ideas and processes**

What melts in the sun?

Asking the open question: what melts in the sun? is a simple way to get children thinking about the melting points of everyday objects and materials during the summer term when, with a bit of luck, we should be able to enjoy some hot, sunny days. A metal muffin tin filled with assorted objects and left outside will allow children to make predictions regarding which materials they think will melt and also how long they think this might take. Careful observations over a period of time could be photographed and an explanation as to why certain materials melted and others did not could be offered. This enquiry activity might also lead to children carrying out their own research into the melting points of everyday materials.

Working scientifically

- **Setting up simple practical enquiries, comparative and fair tests**
- **Making systematic and careful observations and, where appropriate, taking accurate measurements using standard units, using a range of equipment, including thermometers and data loggers**
- **Recording findings using simple scientific language, drawings, labelled diagrams, keys, bar charts and tables**
- **Identifying differences, similarities or changes related to simple scientific ideas and processes**

Research it

Older readers of this book might remember a popular television game show called 'Play Your Cards Right' whereby contestants had to predict whether the value of a playing card would be higher or lower than the previous one dealt to them. Children will have great fun measuring or researching the freezing or melting points of a range of everyday objects and materials and then presenting this information, following the format of the game, for a partner to try their luck at. An example of this might be 'Play Your Melting Points Right':

- Ice melts at 0°C – the next card says 'butter'. Do you think the melting point of butter is higher or lower than the melting point of ice?
- Butter melts at 50°C – the next card says 'wax'. Do you think the melting point of wax is higher or lower than the melting point of butter?
- And so on... until at least six different cards have been turned over and the melting points have been predicted and evaluated.

> Working scientifically
> - **Asking relevant questions and using different types of scientific enquiries to answer them**
> - **Gathering, recording, classifying and presenting data in a variety of ways to help in answering questions**
> - **They should also recognise when and how secondary sources might help them to answer questions that cannot be answered through practical investigations (non-statutory notes and guidance)**

Statutory Requirement: identify the part played by evaporation and condensation in the water cycle and associate the rate of evaporation with temperature.

There are some brilliant water cycle songs and raps to be found on the internet – singing and learning these will help children to consolidate tricky vocabulary such as evaporation and condensation (also precipitation if you are being adventurous!). Remember to link science learning to genres of writing too whereby children could imagine themselves as one single rain drop and then describe the journey they would take through the water cycle from puddle to sea to cloud to rain and back to puddle again.

Modelling the water cycle (1)

A really effective way for children to see evaporation and condensation in action is to pour hot water into a clear bowl and then cover the bowl with cling film and secure this tightly. Place a few ice cubes in the centre of the cling film and observe how the hot water begins to evaporate as a gas in an upwards direction but then cools on contact with the cling film, turns back to liquid and drips down into the bowl again.

This activity offers a simple and visual way to explain the often invisible process of the water cycle. Children should make links between their models and how, in real-life, water from oceans and lakes is warmed by the sun and evaporates as water vapour (gas) up into the sky. Water vapour eventually cools down or condenses to form water droplets which, in turn, form clouds. When the water droplets become too heavy, they fall back to the ground as rain, snow or hail (we call this part: precipitation).

Modelling the water cycle (2)

Making a 'window water cycle' is my new favourite activity for modelling the process of evaporation and condensation in a way that makes the water cycle meaningful and accessible for children. Each child should draw a scene which includes sun, clouds and lake or sea on the front of a transparent sealable bag, using a permanent pen. Next, they should add some blue food colouring to half a cup of water, and pour this into the bag up to the water level they have drawn and then seal the bag tightly. Using strong tape, stick the bag directly onto the classroom window in direct sunlight and observe over the day how the water warms up and evaporates into water vapour (the bag will appear misty) and then cools back to a liquid and drips down again, with the appearance of rain (this works especially well when children lightly press at the top of the bag).

Children should be able to label evaporation and condensation on their scene as well as explain to a partner what is happening at each stage. An open thinking question such as, 'How is your water cycle the same or different to the real water cycle?' makes a great discussion point and assessment strategy.

Note: this activity works most successfully on a warm, sunny day.

Working scientifically

- **Gathering, recording, classifying and presenting data in a variety of ways to help in answering questions**
- **Recording findings using simple scientific language, drawings, labelled diagrams, keys, bar charts and tables**
- **Identifying differences, similarities or changes related to simple scientific ideas and processes**

Creative post-topic assessment

Ask children to draw a 'word art' whereby they present key words from this topic, such as solid, liquid, gas, melting, freezing, evaporation, condensation and water cycle, in a decorative style that interprets the actual process being named. The word 'melt' could be drawn so that individual letters look like they are dripping and turning to liquid, with a pool collecting below, or the phrase 'water cycle' could be presented so that the letters take the shape of a circle with some of them 'evaporating' upwards whilst others have formed water droplets and appear to be 'raining' in a downwards direction. Word art is a superb way of collecting assessment evidence whereby children's understanding of the words and processes involved is reflected in the choices they make to present these.

> Working scientifically
> - **Gathering, recording, classifying and presenting data in a variety of ways to help in answering questions**
> - **Identifying differences, similarities or changes related to simple scientific ideas and processes**

Properties and Changes of Materials in Year 5

In my humble opinion, some of the statutory objectives for this topic feel a little muddled and so I have separated statements out within objectives to give the unit of work a greater feeling of continuity and flow. Parts of statements highlighted in bold are the ones being covered by the activities beneath each one.

> **Statutory Requirement: compare and group together everyday materials on the basis of their properties, including their hardness**, solubility, **transparency, conductivity (electrical and thermal), and response to magnets.**

Children in Year 1 and Year 2 will have had plenty of opportunities for materials testing. Some common Key Stage 1 investigations involve children working scientifically to find the most waterproof, absorbent, stretchy, see through or protective materials (as described on page 79). In Year 3, hardness tests may have been covered when investigating the physical properties of rock samples (see page 100) as well as transparency tests using data logging equipment or light meters during the topic of 'Light' (see page 107) and finding out how materials respond to magnets in the 'Forces and Magnets' topic (see page 123). Children in Year 4 will have carried out electrical conductivity investigations during the 'Electricity' topic (see page 135), therefore, it is vital that Year 5 teachers do not simply repeat what has already been carried out in previous years.

An effective way to facilitate progression in conceptual understanding and skills is to start by placing a wide range of objects and materials on children's tables and then ask each group to generate as many different property words as they can think of to build up a whole-class 'properties' word bank. Children could suggest opposites (antonyms) to property words too so that the list contains examples such as hard/soft, stretchy/not stretchy, bouncy/not bouncy, shiny/dull, rough/smooth, flexible/rigid, waterproof/not waterproof, absorbent/not absorbent, opaque/transparent/translucent, magnetic/non magnetic, electrical conductor/electrical insulator, thermal conductor/thermal insulator, strong/fragile and so on.

Children could also record these property words by writing directly or sticking labels onto samples of different materials, for example, a sheet of aluminium foil might have labels with property words such as:

not stretchy, shiny, flexible, not absorbent, non-magnetic, opaque etc. all over it. This makes an excellent assessment tool at the start of the topic to reveal children's understanding of properties of materials as well as an effective display in the classroom.

To extend this further, each group could be asked to choose one property word from the bank, e.g. magnetic, and then plan and carry out their own fair test investigation in order to find out more about this property using the objects and materials already provided plus any additional items they might request. Children should then compare and group together their materials according to the results they have obtained. By organising and introducing the activity in this way, children are given opportunities to formulate their own questions and feel motivated to pursue their own lines of enquiry.

Some creative examples of further materials tests are:

Response to magnets

Do magnets work through different liquids? How could we test this? Does the viscosity (thickness) of a liquid affect magnetism? Is it possible to stop the force of magnetism? How does the type of material wrapped around a magnet or the number of layers affect the number of paper clips picked up?

Thermal conductivity

Which cup keeps my drink hot for the longest time? Which container is best for stopping my ice-cream from melting? Which material is best for keeping a jacket potato hot? Which is the best hand warmer?

Investigate how penguins keep warm in cold climates: What happens to the temperature of hot water in a small pop bottle when it stands alone compared to when it is surrounded by other small pop bottles containing the same amount of hot water?

Absorbency

Which is the most absorbent brand of rabbit bedding, nappy or kitchen towel? What happens when we place a sugar cube in a shallow dish of food colouring? What happens if I add more sugar cubes to make a tower? Can I put a layer of material in between two sugar cubes to stop absorbency? Which material works best?

Stretch-ability

What length of different types of elastic do I need for an 'action man' doll to bungee jump safely? Which material is best to use for a tug of war? Which is the stretchiest material I can use for a new superhero costume?

Working scientifically

- **Planning different types of scientific enquiries to answer questions, including recognising and controlling variables where necessary**
- **Taking measurements, using a range of scientific equipment, with increasing accuracy and precision, taking repeat readings when appropriate**
- **Recording data and results of increasing complexity using scientific diagrams and labels, classification keys, tables, scatter graphs, bar and line graphs**

- **Using test results to make predictions to set up further comparative and fair tests**
- **Reporting and presenting findings from enquiries, including conclusions, causal relationships and explanations of and degree of trust in results, in oral and written forms such as displays and other presentations**

> **Statutory Requirement:** give reasons, based on evidence from comparative and fair tests, for the particular uses of everyday materials, including metals, wood and plastic.

Groups should use the results from their own comparative and fair tests as described above to explain why particular materials are chosen and used for different purposes. This gives children a chance to describe the tests they have carried out and share the outcomes of their investigations with each other.

Working scientifically

- **Reporting and presenting findings from enquiries, including conclusions, causal relationships and explanations of and degree of trust in results, in oral and written forms such as displays and other presentations**
- **Identifying scientific evidence that has been used to support or refute ideas or arguments**

> **Statutory Requirement: compare and group together everyday materials on the basis of their properties, including their** hardness, **solubility,** transparency, conductivity (electrical and thermal), and response to magnets
> **Statutory Requirement: understand that some materials will dissolve in liquid to form a solution,** and describe how to recover a substance from a solution

Which materials in my kitchen cupboard dissolve?

As an introduction to dissolving, present groups of children with a number of solids found in a kitchen cupboard and ask them simply to observe and record what happens when they add their selected solid to water. The solids could include different kinds of sugar (including icing sugar), different kinds of salt, flour, milkshake powder, instant hot chocolate, coffee, tea leaves from inside a tea bag, instant soup, peppercorns, mini marshmallows, jelly crystals, 'hundreds and thousands' and popping candy.

Children should make comparisons between the solids that can be seen floating in or on the surface of the water (and could be scooped out again with a spoon) and the solids that seem to have disappeared or dissolved into the water (and can no longer be scooped out with a spoon). They could record the results of their investigation by sorting and grouping the solutions or mixtures into soluble and insoluble categories and then suggesting other solids to test and categorise in the same way.

Alternative solubility investigations

Children should be encouraged to ask their own solubility questions and pursue lines of enquiry to investigate for themselves. Some examples might include: Which type of sugar dissolves fastest in my cup of tea? What happens when I pour water over Skittles sweets in a shallow dish? What happens to different sized cubes when I add hot water to make jelly? Does stirring affect how quickly a solid dissolves? Does salt dissolve in liquids other than water? Is there a limit to how much solid will dissolve? What does the temperature of the water need to be in order to dissolve marshmallows?

Note: Aim to include a range of liquids, other than just water, if at all possible. An intriguing teacher demonstration could be how nail varnish remover containing acetone dissolves an expanded polystyrene cup on immediate contact.

Working scientifically

- **Planning different types of scientific enquiries to answer questions, including recognising and controlling variables where necessary**
- **Taking measurements, using a range of scientific equipment, with increasing accuracy and precision, taking repeat readings when appropriate**
- **Recording data and results of increasing complexity using scientific diagrams and labels, classification keys, tables, scatter graphs, bar and line graphs**
- **Using test results to make predictions to set up further comparative and fair tests**
- **Reporting and presenting findings from enquiries, including conclusions, causal relationships and explanations of and degree of trust in results, in oral and written forms such as displays and other presentations**

Statutory Requirement: understand that some materials will dissolve in liquid to form a solution, and **describe how to recover a substance from a solution.**

Finding a solution solution!

Using the mixtures and solutions created in the activities above, children could be challenged to separate the solids from the liquids again. They should be encouraged to use a range of filtering equipment and explore how the solids that have dissolved cannot be recovered using a sieve or filter paper. Children could try evaporating the liquid in different ways, such as by placing solutions on a sunny window spot or warm radiator, leaving them at room temperature in the classroom and also by safely heating a small amount on a stove or by using a heat stand or oil burner with a tea light candle. Thinking about and investigating evaporation rates has good links to work already carried out in the 'States of Matter' topic whereby Year 4 children associate the rate of evaporation with temperature (see page 86).

- **Reporting and presenting findings from enquiries, including conclusions, causal relationships and explanations of and degree of trust in results, in oral and written forms such as displays and other presentations**

> **Statutory Requirement:** use knowledge of solids, liquids and gases to decide how mixtures might be separated, including through filtering, sieving and evaporating.

Challenge activities

Open-ended challenge activities enable children to use and apply what they have learnt about dissolving, mixing, sieving, filtering and evaporating. Popular and motivating contexts include separating ingredients from unusual mixtures such as a witch's brew, unconventional recipe, dirty contaminated water sample or mixed materials found at the scene of a fictitious crime. Mixtures provided might include something magnetic (such as paper clips), a number of insoluble solids of different sized particles (such as dried peas, rice and sand) something soluble (such as sugar or salt) and an unidentified (and perhaps coloured) liquid.

Children should decide for themselves how to separate the ingredients, what equipment to use and the order of processes involved. They should be allowed to trial their ideas and report on how well they achieved the desired outcome, including what they might be able to do to improve their chosen method or perhaps why they were not successful this time. The challenge is a perfect way to assess children's understanding of the processes involved at the start of the topic and then revisited later with an opportunity for them to evaluate, adapt and refine their thinking.

Working scientifically

- **Planning different types of scientific enquiries to answer questions, including recognising and controlling variables where necessary**
- **Reporting and presenting findings from enquiries, including conclusions, causal relationships and explanations of and degree of trust in results, in oral and written forms such as displays and other presentations**

Separating solids and liquids in a recipe for lemonade

Children could be given the recipe for a new lemonade drink to make and taste. As they add a range of ingredients to warm water, they should identify which ones do and do not dissolve and explain how each one could be recovered if too much of it had been added.

Groups working together should pour two pints of warm water into a large transparent jug or pitcher and then squeeze the juice of half a lemon into the water to observe how the juice dissolves in the water but any pips or flesh do not (these should be removed with a sieve before continuing). Next, they should add six tablespoons of sugar and stir before adding half a tablespoon of food-grade citric acid crystals (bought at supermarkets, chemists, home-brew suppliers or the internet) and stir again. Children should observe that both of these ingredients dissolve in the water and so they would need to evaporate the water away in order to recover them together from solution.

Finally, children could add chopped lemons or grated lemon rind to their drink and observe that these do not dissolve and could be separated using different grades of filter. Jugs of lemonade should be placed in a fridge to cool before tasting. Creative links to the English curriculum might include children providing the drinks company with a taste test review to let them know what might be improved.

Working scientifically

- **Reporting and presenting findings from enquiries, including conclusions, causal relationships and explanations of and degree of trust in results, in oral and written forms such as displays and other presentations**

> **Statutory Requirement:** demonstrate that dissolving, mixing and changes of state are reversible changes.

The drinks company from the lemonade activity described above have contacted the class again to find out whether or not it is possible to freeze small pieces of fruit and water in order to make fruity ice cubes. They would ideally like lemon ice cubes to go with their new lemonade drink but are wondering if other types of fruit freeze more quickly and take longer to melt when placed into a drink.

Children can work in small groups to plan their investigations using a range of chopped fruit such as lemon, strawberry, apple, banana and grape. They should find out how long it takes for different types of fruit to freeze when added to water in an ice cube tray and placed in a freezer. They should also investigate how long different cubes take to melt when added to a drink.

Finally, the company are updating their handbook of scientific skills and would like to know which of the processes used in making the fruity ice cubes and the previous activity of making lemonade can be reversed. Children should think about the skills of mixing, dissolving, melting and freezing and decide whether or not the solids and liquids could be changed back again in each example.

Working scientifically

- **Planning different types of scientific enquiries to answer questions, including recognising and controlling variables where necessary**
- **Taking measurements, using a range of scientific equipment, with increasing accuracy and precision, taking repeat readings when appropriate**
- **Recording data and results of increasing complexity using scientific diagrams and labels, classification keys, tables, scatter graphs, bar and line graphs**
- **Using test results to make predictions to set up further comparative and fair tests**
- **Reporting and presenting findings from enquiries, including conclusions, causal relationships and explanations of and degree of trust in results, in oral and written forms such as displays and other presentations**

> **Statutory Requirement:** explain that some changes result in the formation of new materials, and that this kind of change is not usually reversible, including changes associated with burning and the action of acid on bicarbonate of soda.

Creating new materials (1)

The ancient tradition of burning paper money during special holidays, such as Chinese New Year, provides a fascinating real-life context in which children can observe what happens when paper is burned. Small groups should investigate under close teacher supervision using a tea light candle or safety lighter, long tongs or pliers and a tray containing sand.

Children should be encouraged to think about why fake money (often called joss paper or ghost money) is used instead of real notes and discuss how, when something is burned, the original material turns to ash and this change cannot usually be reversed.

Working scientifically

- **Reporting and presenting findings from enquiries, including conclusions, causal relationships and explanations of and degree of trust in results, in oral and written forms such as displays and other presentations**
- **Identifying scientific evidence that has been used to support or refute ideas or arguments**

Creating new materials (2)

Children of any age love mixing bicarbonate of soda with weak acid such as lemon juice or vinegar and then observing an exciting chemical reaction involving bubbles, foam and, possibly, an overflowing container. A fun way to show that a new substance is being created is to try and capture the otherwise invisible carbon dioxide gas that is being produced.

Children will take great delight in inflating a balloon on top of a bottle or a thin rubber glove stretched over the neck of an empty jam jar. They should attempt to explain how the bicarbonate of soda and vinegar have reacted together to form a new material and that the original materials can no longer (or not easily) be recovered.

Year 5 children could use this activity as a context for asking further questions, making predictions and setting up their own comparative and fair tests. Examples might include:

Does the amount of vinegar affect the size of the inflated balloon? What other liquids would I be able to try safely? Can I inflate a paper bag in the same way? If I change the amount of bicarbonate of soda what will happen to how quickly the glove inflates?

Note: safety glasses should be worn if at all possible during these activities to avoid vinegar or similar substances splashing into children's eyes.

- **Using test results to make predictions to set up further comparative and fair tests**
- **Reporting and presenting findings from enquiries, including conclusions, causal relationships and explanations of and degree of trust in results, in oral and written forms such as displays and other presentations**
- **Identifying scientific evidence that has been used to support or refute ideas or arguments**

Can we make fizzy lemonade?

Children could experiment with the original lemonade recipe (described earlier in this topic on page 95) in an attempt to make it fizzy. They should think about which edible ingredient could be added to the drink to create carbon dioxide gas. Groups working together could try adding a teaspoon of different ingredients such as icing sugar, castor sugar, self-raising flour, bicarbonate of soda and powdered yeast to a cup containing a small amount of lemon juice and then observe what happens. Children should find that, by adding bicarbonate of soda, they can enjoy an alternative version of the drink which contains bubbles.

Working scientifically

- **Planning different types of scientific enquiries to answer questions, including recognising and controlling variables where necessary**
- **Using test results to make predictions to set up further comparative and fair tests**

7
A Creative Approach to Teaching Rocks

The topic of 'Rocks' is often referred to as the least favourite amongst primary teachers, reporting on time spent searching for new inspiration in an attempt to make lessons more interesting to plan and teach. My approach is to consider and refer to children as geologists as they embark on an exciting study of rocks, fossils and soil. There should be plenty of opportunities for them to discover, handle and investigate for themselves – some children of this age have rock and fossil collections at home and they should be encouraged to bring these in to share and explore with the rest of the class. There are also creative links to history topics such as the Stone age, whereby classic texts such as *Stig of the Dump* by Clive King or *Stone Age Boy* by Satoshi Kitamura can help nurture children's knowledge of rocks in a more meaningful context. One final link, not to be ignored, is that to the popular electronic game of Minecraft. In recent years, I have met many a Year 4 child who can confidently reference rocks such as granite, quartz and obsidian and describe their properties as a result of building in this virtual landscape!

Rocks in Year 3

Statutory Requirement: compare and group together different kinds of rocks on the basis of their appearance and simple physical properties.

Comparing and grouping rocks by appearance

It makes an exciting start to the topic for children to arrive in class to find a mixture of unlabelled rocks (such as marble, granite, sandstone, basalt, slate, clay, chalk, pumice and limestone) displayed on their tables. Working in small groups, they should look carefully at the physical appearance of the samples provided, using hand lenses, microscopes and visualisers if possible, and begin to create a geologist's word bank of the property descriptions generated during this task. Key vocabulary might include: smooth, rough, speckled, grainy, crystals, crumbly, shimmery, translucent, shiny, dull and so on.

Each group should choose an interesting property word from the 'bank' and use this as their criteria for grouping, sorting and classifying the rocks. Can groups guess correctly how others have decided to sort their samples? Have groups only sorted into two distinct categories or are any classifications overlapping? Photographs should be taken, accompanied by children's descriptions of the rocks, and kept as evidence for this objective.

Teachers should ask if children are able to name any of the rocks rather than presuming that they cannot – some will be able to identify common rocks like chalk, slate and granite. Groups or pairs could be provided with a simple key to follow using yes/no questions and identify each type of rock for themselves.

Working scientifically

- **Making systematic and careful observations using a range of equipment**
- **Gathering, recording, classifying and presenting data in a variety of ways to help in answering questions**
- **Recording findings using simple scientific language, drawings, labelled diagrams, keys, bar charts and tables**

Comparing and grouping rocks by physical properties

Children should work in role, as geologists, with the task of investigating the simple physical properties of rocks. Encourage them to use the names of the rocks (introduced in the previous activity) and then work around the following four scenarios:

1. We need to choose a hard rock for a kitchen worktop that will resist scratching – children could carefully scratch each sample using a nail or golf tee and then compare and group rocks according to hardness. There is a great link here to the work of German mineralogist Friedrich Mohs whereby children could even devise their own 'Mohs scale' of hardness using the rock samples provided and the results of their investigation.

2. We need to choose a heard wearing, durable rock for some stone steps or a skate ramp – children could rub each rock an agreed number of times using sand paper and then compare and group rocks according to durability.

3. We need to choose a waterproof rock for the roof of a new building – children could drip water onto each rock using a pipette before comparing and grouping rocks according to permeability.

4. We need to choose a rock that will not react with acid in rain for a statue in the park – children could place rocks into separate containers containing a measured amount of white vinegar. They should compare and group them according to how much they reacted with the vinegar to produce bubbles of gas.

Working scientifically

- **Setting up simple practical enquiries, comparative and fair tests**
- **Making systematic and careful observations**
- **Gathering, recording, classifying and presenting data in a variety of ways to help in answering questions**
- **Recording findings using simple scientific language, drawings, labelled diagrams, keys, bar charts and tables**

- **Reporting on findings from enquiries, including oral and written explanations, displays or presentations of results and conclusions**
- **Using results to draw simple conclusions, make predictions for new values, suggest improvements and raise further questions**

I-spy rocks

It is vital that children relate the small samples of rock they have observed and investigated in the classroom with rocks all around them in the real world. A simple pictorial 'I-spy' sheet could be created using photographs and names of the rocks used in previous activities so that children can get out and about, make notes and observational sketches to record where they can see these rocks, what they are being used for and why.

Working scientifically

- **Making systematic and careful observations**
- **Gathering, recording, classifying and presenting data in a variety of ways to help in answering questions**
- **Recording findings using simple scientific language, drawings, labelled diagrams, keys, bar charts and tables**

Statutory Requirement: describe in simple terms how fossils are formed when things that have lived are trapped within rock.

Children will enjoy modelling how fossils are formed by making different types of fossil and then drawing upon their experiences to describe these processes in simple terms.

The following activities should link directly to the 'Evolution and Inheritance' topic in Year 6 (as described on page 67) whereby children learn that fossils provide information about living things that inhabited the Earth millions of years ago.

Make a mould fossil

A mould forms when an organism sinks to the sea floor and is pressed into layers of sediment (earth, rock, sand, plants, mud etc). As the layers build up and the pressure increases, the sediment turns to hard rock. Over time, the organism gradually rots away and disappears. This leaves an imprint, like a mould, of its original shape.

How to make a simple mould fossil: mix 1 cup of flour, ¼ cup coffee granules, ½ cup salt (to represent the layers of sediment) and ½ cup water (to represent sea water) in a large bowl to make a dough. Take a piece of the dough and flatten it out with your hand to represent the earth/rock. Choose an object from nature such as a bone, shell, feather, leaf, flower, claw, tooth or even a mini plastic dinosaur toy and press this into the dough. Carefully, remove the object and take a look at the mould that was made. Now let your imprinted 'fossil' dry out.

Make a cast fossil

A cast fossil is made when minerals and sediment fill in the spaces left behind when an organism buried in the rock has rotted away and disappeared. This makes an exact replica (or cast) of the original organism.

How to make a simple cast fossil: cut the top off a paper cup so that it is around 5 cm tall and then fill this three quarters full with clay, pressing it in firmly to the sides and the bottom. Take your natural object (as in the previous mould fossil activity) and press it upside down and carefully into the clay. Remove the object and check that the imprint is clear. Make a thick mixture of plaster of Paris and water in a separate cup and pour this evenly on top of the imprint you have made in the clay. Let the plaster set and then rip off the paper cup and carefully separate your clay mould from the plaster cast.

Make an amber fossil

Tiny creatures can become trapped in sticky tree resin. Over many years, this becomes hard and forms stone called amber. In some pieces of amber you can find the remains of organisms perfectly preserved.

How to make a simple amber fossil: use an old cheese grater to slice a yellow or orange candle into small pieces of coloured wax. Scoop around four teaspoons of wax into a clear, strong sandwich bag and seal the bag before dunking it in a jug of very hot water for around one minute. Remove the bag and observe that the heat from the water has melted the wax into a liquid state. Carefully open the bag and drop in a small plastic creature, such as an insect (sourced on the internet or in a joke kit). After a few more minutes, the liquid wax will cool and solidify, trapping the creature and preserving it as though in a fossilised form.

> Working scientifically
> - **Reporting on findings from enquiries, including oral and written explanations, displays or presentations of results and conclusions**
> - **Using straightforward scientific evidence to answer questions or to support their findings**

Statutory Requirement: recognise that soils are made from rocks and organic matter.

Children should be able to describe the process of how rocks change into soil through weathering and erosion over many years. More creative methods will help children to embed their understanding of how soil is formed, examples of this include as a narrative, cartoon strip, rap, animation, drama or dance.

- **Gathering, recording, classifying and presenting data in a variety of ways to help in answering questions**
- **Identifying differences, similarities or changes related to simple scientific ideas and processes**

Separating soil

Children could look at samples of different soil using a hand lens or under a microscope (ten times magnification will show larger mineral particles as well as fragments of small rocks and of organic matter) in order to identify for themselves what it is made from.

Adding water to a sample of soil (around one third soil to two thirds water in a clean jam jar or pop bottle with the top cut off), will allow children to make careful observations over a period of time, such as a morning or afternoon. They should first look for bubbles of air escaping from the soil before stirring or shaking the mixture and leaving it to settle and separate out into different layers of sand, pebbles, silt, clay and organic matter (either dissolved or floating at the top). Children could compare different soils from home, school and garden centres by making measurements of the height of each layer and learning about how soils vary. Don't forget to take photographs of the separating soil activity for children to label and keep as evidence of their understanding.

Another creative way for children to record their observations is to challenge them to make a model showing the separated layers using different coloured Lego™ blocks.

Working scientifically

- **Setting up simple practical enquiries, comparative and fair tests**
- **Making systematic and careful observations and, where appropriate, taking accurate measurements using standard units, using a range of equipment, including thermometers and data loggers**
- **Recording findings using simple scientific language, drawings, labelled diagrams, keys, bar charts and tables**

Physics

8
A Creative Approach to Teaching Light

Children may have carried out simple tests in Key Stage 1 'Materials' topics, such as to find out which material is best for making bedroom curtains or a sleep mask, however, for many, Year 3 is the first time they will be asked to consider what light is, how it travels and how it can be reflected and blocked. In Year 6, their learning will be extended as they gain a deeper understanding of how we see things and shadow formation.

Light in Year 3

> **Statutory Requirement:** recognise that they need light in order to see things and that dark is the absence of light.

In order to teach the concept that we need light in order to see, there is no better way than to take children deep underground or into a dark cave! Being able to recreate this scenario is extremely difficult in a primary school – even the darkest of cupboards is likely to have light creeping under the door. Try blocking this light using blackout sheets, black sacks and draft excluders to enable children to experience complete darkness for themselves.

Asking questions such as: What can you see? Why do you think this? What will you need in order to see? will help children to formulate their scientific ideas.

Note: If children can see anything at all in the dark space you have created then the activity will be null and void, only serving to confirm any misconceptions children might have.

Working scientifically

- **Identifying differences, similarities or changes related to simple scientific ideas and processes**
- **Using straightforward scientific evidence to answer questions or to support their findings**

Sorting light sources

Refer back to the previous activity and ask children what they would need to enable them to see in complete darkness. Answers describing light sources only serve to confirm that we need light in order to see things. Present small groups with a range of objects such as a shiny Christmas bauble, aluminium foil, reflective arm band, mirror, electric tea light (switched on), tube of glitter, a crystal, pocket torch (switched on) and a phone or electronic device (switched on) then ask children to sort the items into which they think give out light and which they think do not.

Each small group working together could be given an empty shoe box with one tiny hole pushed through with a pin in one end only. Children take turns to place one object at a time inside the box, put the lid on and then look through the tiny hole into the box. Ask: What can you see when you look into the box? For most of the objects there will be complete darkness, however, a genuine light source will show light in the box. Children may need to re-sort and group the objects into 'light source' and 'not light source' as a result of what they have found out, with some potential surprises!

Working scientifically

- **Setting up simple practical enquiries, comparative and fair tests**
- **Gathering, recording, classifying and presenting data in a variety of ways to help in answering questions**
- **Recording findings using simple scientific language, drawings, labelled diagrams, keys, bar charts and tables**

Statutory Requirement: notice that light is reflected from surfaces.

Children should understand that light is reflected from most surfaces, not just shiny or bright ones, albeit in different amounts. The light sensor on a data logger is an essential piece of kit when teaching such a concept whereby children can measure light being reflected from a range of surfaces and, generate an actual reading of reflected light (in lux). They can learn for themselves that no material they are using has a reading of zero, but some measurements are extremely high compared to others that are low. Materials such as different coloured card or paper, aluminium foil, brown parcel paper, plastic bag, laminated paper, mirror, corrugated card, carpet and sponge are great for asking children to predict which they think will be good or poor reflectors of light and why they think this.

My favourite science lesson of recent months was taught within an Ancient Greeks history theme. Groups of children were challenged to find the most reflective material for Perseus' shield in order to defeat the Gorgon, Medusa. Based on their results after investigating with a data logger, children chose the most reflective material to line the back of a cardboard shield and then use this to protect themselves from a moving, talking model of Medusa with glowing eyes (bought from the internet) and prevent themselves from being turned to stone!

Working scientifically

- **Asking relevant questions and using different types of scientific enquiries to answer them**
- **Setting up simple practical enquiries, comparative and fair tests**
- **Making systematic and careful observations and, where appropriate, taking accurate measurements using standard units, using a range of equipment, including thermometers and data loggers**
- **Using straightforward scientific evidence to answer questions or to support their findings**

Statutory Requirement: recognise that light from the sun can be dangerous and that there are ways to protect their eyes.

Aim to carry out this activity during the summer term when children can investigate ways in which they can protect themselves from sunlight whilst learning and playing outdoors. There are some interesting activities to be explored using colour changing UV beads (bought cheaply from the internet) and these would progress perfectly from activities described on pages 65-66 when Year 1 children learn about sunshine and summer time during the topic of 'Seasonal Changes'.

The indicator beads change colour when exposed to ultra violet light so could be used to test the effectiveness of sunscreen or to see how well UV light is blocked out by filters in sunglasses. Children could place an agreed number of beads into a clear, sealable bag and then apply a different strength sunscreen to the outside of each bag before leaving them in direct sunlight. After ten minutes, they should examine the beads carefully to see how much they have changed colour. Remember to set up one 'control' bag without any sunscreen coating for comparison purposes.

Children could also test the ability of different sunglasses to block out ultraviolet light by covering a few beads with the lens of different sunglasses or a range of transparent materials when placed in direct sunlight. They should make simple conclusions that, if the beads do not change colour, the lens or material is blocking out harmful ultraviolet light and providing protection from the sun.

Working scientifically

- **Asking relevant questions and using different types of scientific enquiries to answer them**
- **Setting up simple practical enquiries, comparative and fair tests**
- **Making systematic and careful observations and, where appropriate, taking accurate measurements using standard units, using a range of equipment, including thermometers and data loggers**

- **Reporting on findings from enquiries, including oral and written explanations, displays or presentations of results and conclusions**
- **Using results to draw simple conclusions, make predictions for new values, suggest improvements and raise further questions**

More data logging

Don't forget, you can also use a data logger with a light sensor (or light sensor app downloaded to an electronic device) to measure the amount of light shining through different transparent materials when they are placed in front of a lit torch. This investigation might be used to answer questions such as, 'Are all sunglasses the same?' or 'How can we protect our eyes from the sun?'. Children could test real sunglasses or make a pair of sunglasses using a cardboard template from a pair of 3D glasses and then use their results to decide which material they should choose to provide the most effective and protective lens.

Working scientifically

- **Setting up simple practical enquiries, comparative and fair tests**
- **Making systematic and careful observations and, where appropriate, taking accurate measurements using standard units, using a range of equipment, including thermometers and data loggers**
- **Using results to draw simple conclusions, make predictions for new values, suggest improvements and raise further questions**
- **Using straightforward scientific evidence to answer questions or to support their findings**

Statutory Requirement: recognise that shadows are formed when the light from a light source is blocked by a solid object.

Children should be given time and freedom to explore shadows for themselves, whether in a darkened room with a selection of light sources or outside on a sunny day. Ask plenty of open-ended thinking questions to help them to formulate their initial ideas, such as: 'What do you need in order to make a shadow?', 'What kind of object makes a good shadow?', 'What do you notice about shadows?'. Children can have all manner of fun creating shadow shapes and puppets using their bodies or easily accessible materials and a light source. They could record the shadows they make by photographing each other's and writing a set of instructions for how to make a shadow. A relevant story book I often use to accompany shadow exploration and to challenge misconceptions is called *Moonbear's Shadow* by Frank Asch.

Shadow sculpture

Give groups of children a large bag of junk modelling materials containing a range of transparent, translucent and opaque objects. An old overhead projector is perfect to use for this activity. Ask children to place objects from the bag onto the OHP screen (switched on) and observe the shapes and shadows that can be created. They should consider if certain kinds of materials make better shadows than others and why this might be.

Try using coloured objects and observe what happens to the colour of the shadow, also investigate what happens when they use objects with patterns and images printed onto the materials and see what happens when in shadow form.

Working scientifically

- **Asking relevant questions and using different types of scientific enquiries to answer them**
- **Using results to draw simple conclusions, make predictions for new values, suggest improvements and raise further questions**
- **Using straightforward scientific evidence to answer questions or to support their findings**

Statutory Requirement: find patterns that determine the size of shadows.

A simple, open-ended question such as: 'Can you make your shadow bigger or smaller?' or 'Is an object's shadow always the same size?' is often all that it takes to get children investigating. Sharing a story book where the main character has been frightened by the shadow of what seems to be an enormous monster can also be a great stimulus for inquisitive minds. In lower Key Stage 2, children should recognise when a simple fair test is necessary and help to decide how to set this up. The pattern seeking investigation described below provides the perfect opportunity for doing so.

The great shadow size investigation: just one possibility!

Working collaboratively in small groups, children could place a large piece of flip chart paper on the table with a lit angle poise lamp at one end (draw around the base of the lamp on the paper to ensure that it stays in exactly the same place throughout). Children could use pre-cut footprint templates that are exactly 10 cm in length and stick the first footprint on the paper so that appears as if someone has taken one step away from the lamp.

They should place a solid object (this could be a Lego or Playmobil™ figure) at the toes of the footprint (10cm away from the light source), observe and then draw around the shadow created before measuring and recording its length in a suitable way, such as in a simple table. Children could now stick another footprint onto the paper, heel to the toe of the previous one; reposition the figure so that it is now two footsteps (20cm) away from the light source. They should draw around it and then measure and record its length again. Repeat this procedure until the figure is some distance away from the light source and children have generated an interesting set of results.

The suggestion of using pre-cut foot-print templates is an attempt to avoid children becoming confused when asked to collect, record and interpret two variables measured in centimetres – the distance away from the light source and the length of the shadow.

Note: More able children will be unlikely to require the foot print templates and could measure distance from light source with a tape measure or metre stick.

Working scientifically

- **Setting up simple practical enquiries, comparative and fair tests**
- **Making systematic and careful observations and, where appropriate, taking accurate measurements using standard units, using a range of equipment, including thermometers and data loggers**
- **Recording findings using simple scientific language, drawings, labelled diagrams, keys, bar charts and tables**
- **Reporting on findings from enquiries, including oral and written explanations, displays or presentations of results and conclusions**
- **Using results to draw simple conclusions, make predictions for new values, suggest improvements and raise further questions**

Light in Year 6

Statutory Requirement: recognise that light appears to travel in straight lines.

Children in Year 6 should be given a period of open-ended exploration to revisit and recap the Year 3 programme of study for 'Light'. A darkened room and some good quality torches is a great starting point whereby children can investigate whether or not light can easily be bent or curved.

They could stand three pieces of thick card, with holes punched into the centre, upright in a row and observe how light from their torch can travel through the holes and shine onto a wall or surface at the other end. They should predict what might happen if they rearrange the cards in an uneven line, or use cards with holes punched in different positions, before observing that the light cannot travel through all three cards as it travels only in straight lines.

Working scientifically

- **Using test results to make predictions to set up further comparative and fair tests**
- **Identifying scientific evidence that has been used to support or refute ideas or arguments**

A common misconception amongst primary aged children is that we see things because light 'shines out' of our eyes as opposed to objects giving out or reflecting light into the eye. A simple way to demonstrate that our eyes do not give out light is to close one eye and then look down a narrow sweets tube with only the lid removed (making sure the eye socket is positioned flush to the entrance of the tube) or to peep through a tiny hole pushed into one end of a shoe box with the lid on tightly. Children should explain why they can only see complete darkness!

Working scientifically

- **Identifying scientific evidence that has been used to support or refute ideas or arguments**

Light maze

Greet children with a tricky challenge set out for them whereby each small group has a large piece of flip chart paper placed on their table, a torch with a strong, narrow beam of light fixed in position at one end of the paper and an upright piece of card with a human eye 'target' printed onto it placed at the other end of the paper but facing away from the torch. Without moving the torch or the target, groups should work together to decide how they could shine the light from the torch into the 'eye'.

After initial exploration, groups may ask for additional materials so that they can reflect the light onto the target. They will need two, three or four mirrors (or other reflective surfaces) depending on where they position them (mirrors can be positioned upright using play-dough or pegs clipped perpendicular to the base of the mirror).

When successful, children should record the path taken by the beam of light travelling from their torch to the target by drawing directly onto the flip chart paper. This provides a visual record for them to show how light travels in straight lines and can be reflected into a target (the eye).

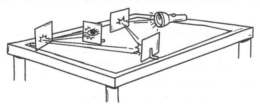

Working scientifically

- **Planning different types of scientific enquiries to answer questions, including recognising and controlling variables where necessary**
- **Recording data and results of increasing complexity using scientific diagrams and labels, classification keys, tables, scatter graphs, bar and line graphs**

- **Reporting and presenting findings from enquiries, including conclusions, causal relationships and explanations of and degree of trust in results, in oral and written forms such as displays and other presentations**

Statutory Requirement: explain that we see things because light travels from light sources to our eyes or from light sources to objects and then to our eyes.

Show children a cuddly toy and ask them to draw a quick diagram on a mini whiteboard to show how they are able to see this. This seemingly simple task provides an enlightening pre-assessment opportunity whereby any remaining misconceptions about how light travels can be uncovered. Compare sketches across the whole class and look for similarities and differences in children's scientific thinking.

Small groups working together could model how we see things by using string to represent the path of light travelling in a straight line from a light source (torch) to an object (cuddly toy) and then to a person's eyes. They should ensure that the string is pulled tight and that it does not curve or bend to provide an inappropriate model. Groups could be challenged further to use the string to show how a person could turn their back to the object (teddy) and use a mirror to view this without looking at it directly.

Working scientifically

- **Recording data and results of increasing complexity using scientific diagrams and labels, classification keys, tables, scatter graphs, bar and line graphs**
- **Identifying scientific evidence that has been used to support or refute ideas or arguments**

Statutory Requirement: use the idea that light travels in straight lines to explain why shadows have the same shape as the objects that cast them.

Year 6 teachers should avoid repeating the activity from Year 3 whereby children investigate how they can change the size of a shadow (described on page 111). Children should have opportunities to recap how shadows are formed and which types of materials can be used to create shadows as well as finding out more about shadow size, shape, colour and whether or not detail/features are visible in shadows.

To focus their learning, children could be challenged to choose an object and then try to alter the shape of its shadow without physically altering the object itself. After exploration and determined perseverance, they should come to the conclusion that this is not actually possible! Can they use their knowledge of how light travels to explain why? A simple explanation is that light travels in straight lines so if we extend the lines from the light source to the edges of the object, we will see that light is blocked only within this outline and so the shadow will always mimic the shape of the object.

Working scientifically

- **Planning different types of scientific enquiries to answer questions, including recognising and controlling variables where necessary**
- **Using test results to make predictions to set up further comparative and fair tests**
- **Reporting and presenting findings from enquiries, including conclusions, causal relationships and explanations of and degree of trust in results, in oral and written forms such as displays and other presentations**
- **Identifying scientific evidence that has been used to support or refute ideas or arguments**

9
A Creative Approach to Teaching Sound

Most science topics in the National Curriculum for England are introduced in Key Stage 1 or lower Key Stage 2 and then revisited and extended before the end of Year 6. The topic on 'Sound' is quite unique as it appears only once! However, strong links to the music curriculum will help children to understand the science behind how sounds are made as well as how to vary volume and pitch, and this should be reinforced in music lessons throughout both Key Stage 1 and Key Stage 2. Opportunities for children to design, make and perform with their own musical instruments should also make reference to the science curriculum, as well as inviting expert musicians into school to play a range of different instruments and demonstrate how sounds can be made and altered.

Sound in Year 4

Teachers could set up a data logger with the sound meter linked to an interactive whiteboard (alternatively, download a free sound meter app to an electronic device and link this up in the same way). Ensure that 'the technology' is hidden from children so that all they see as they arrive in the classroom is an ever fluctuating number or dial on the screen. Ask them to suggest what the changing numbers could represent. Why are they increasing and decreasing and what could be controlling this?

Children should discover that the numbers are a measurement of sound (in decibels), more specifically the noises made in and around the classroom! Ask children if it is possible to achieve a sound measurement of zero decibels and why do they think this. This activity is a great way for children to identify the sounds around them and understand that sounds can be measured.

Working scientifically

- **Making systematic and careful observations and, where appropriate, taking accurate measurements using standard units, using a range of equipment, including thermometers and data loggers**
- **Identifying differences, similarities or changes related to simple scientific ideas and processes**

Statutory Requirement: identify how sounds are made, associating some of them with something vibrating.

Vibration stations (1)

Children should understand that sound is made when something vibrates. The vibrations travel through a medium, usually the air, to your ears. This concept can be difficult to teach and understand as we cannot see these vibrations! It is our job to try and make the effects of vibrations visible in some way by planning a range of carefully selected, intriguing activities for children to have fun with and also identify what is actually vibrating in each example.

Activities to include could be:

1 Hold your fingers over your throat when you talk or hum and feel your vocal chords vibrating as they make a sound.

2 Hit a tuning fork on something solid and then touch it gently to a ping pong ball hanging down from a length of string. The ball with bounce backwards and forwards and this shows that the ends of the tuning fork are vibrating as it makes a sound.

3 Hit a tuning fork again and place the ends lightly onto the surface of a shallow bowl of water. The ends of the tuning fork are vibrating and we can see the effect of these vibrations rippling out in every direction on the water, just as sound travels out in every direction to our ears.

4 Place two drums about 30 cm apart. Sprinkle rice on the surface of one drum and then bang the other drum. Observe the rice jump about as the vibrations from the drum being played travel through the air and move them around. How else can you make the rice move without actually touching it or the drum?

Children should experience the full range of activities in order to secure their understanding of how vibrations make sound. They could choose their two favourite activities to take photographs of and annotate them in order to record their understanding of what is actually vibrating and how the sound is being made in each example.

Working scientifically

- **Asking relevant questions and using different types of scientific enquiries to answer them**

- **Making systematic and careful observations and, where appropriate, taking accurate measurements using standard units**

- **Recording findings using simple scientific language, drawings, labelled diagrams, keys, bar charts and tables**

Statutory Requirement: recognise that vibrations from sounds travel through a medium to the ear.

Reverse thinking

The activities prior to this lesson will help children to understand that sound vibrations travel through the air (a gas) in order to reach our ears. Extend children's thinking to consider what would happen if there was no air, such as in a special room where all the air has been removed (a vacuum chamber) or on the surface of the Moon. A Year 4 child, who can explain that 'if there was no air for vibrations to travel through, we would not hear the sounds', is clearly working at the expected standard for this objective. Again there are some fascinating clips on the internet of sounds fading as the air is being pumped out of containers such as bell jars.

Vibration stations (2)

More fun and practical activities to enable children to experience how sound travels through a medium to the ear will help to secure their understanding of this concept and embedded learning. Examples to include could be:

1 Scratch gently under the table with your finger nail and listen to how loud the sound is. Now scratch again but put your ear to the table and it will sound much louder. Why do you think this is? (Sound vibrations travel much better through a solid, such as wood, than through the air.)

2 Why do people put their ear to a glass against the wall in order to hear the sounds being made next door? Give it a try and what do you find? (Sound vibrations travel much better through a solid, such as glass, than through a gas, such as the air.)

3 Can you explain the phrase: 'Keep your ear to the ground'? (American Indians did this to feel and listen for the vibrations of herds of animals or the approach of their enemy riding on horseback.)

4 String telephones, made using food cans or yoghurt pots, are an old favourite to show children how the vibrations travel along a solid (the string) to allow you to hear sounds that might be too far away to hear when travelling through air.

5 It is tricky to get children listening to sounds travelling through liquids but they can start by thinking about sounds they hear when under water, for example in the swimming pool. They could make their own hydrophone by cutting the bottom off a plastic bottle and submerging this end in a bucket of water. Then, using it to listen beneath the surface when a partner bangs two metal spoons together under the water. Children should compare this to the sounds made out of the water (sounds are louder and clearer under water as vibrations travel better through liquids than in air).

Children could record their understanding by producing activity cards to accompany their favourite examples. Encourage children to write for an audience and a purpose by telling them that their explanations will be used in a science exhibit, show or museum to help other children learn about sound and how vibrations travel.

Working scientifically

- **Reporting on findings from enquiries, including oral and written explanations, displays or presentations of results and conclusions**
- **Using straightforward scientific evidence to answer questions or to support their findings**

> **Statutory Requirement:** find patterns between the pitch of a sound and the features of the object that produced it.

Allow children the freedom to engage in open-ended exploration and formulate their own ideas about pitch. Be brave and empty out the music cupboard, you could be amazed at the weird and wonderful instruments lurking in there, uncovered for years! Some examples of instruments to include could be: chime bars, xylophone, glockenspiel, recorder, swanee whistle, drums, guitar, wind chimes, boom whackers, pan pipes, water pipes and so on. These can all be used to demonstrate that a long or large object vibrating will produce a low pitched sound (they vibrate more slowly) whereas a short or small object vibrating will produce a high pitched sound (they vibrate more quickly).

Don't forget to include activities such as a twanging a ruler over the end of a table, plucking different thicknesses of rubber bands and blowing over glass bottles filled with different amounts of water. Encourage children to think about what is vibrating in each instance and create their own comparative statements, such as 'The longer the chime bar, the lower the sound' or 'The shorter the boom whacker, the higher the sound'.

Working scientifically

- **Making systematic and careful observations**
- **Reporting on findings from enquiries, including oral and written explanations, displays or presentations of results and conclusions**
- **Using results to draw simple conclusions, make predictions for new values, suggest improvements and raise further questions**

> **Statutory Requirement:** find patterns between the volume of a sound and the strength of the vibrations that produced it.

In the context of learning about sound, children might relate the word 'volume' to a button they would press on a remote control to increase or decrease the sound on a television or music system. A creative introductory activity is to point a real remote control at the class (giant ones are great for this) and ask them to increase and decrease the volume of the sounds they are making as you press the 'arrow up' or 'arrow down' buttons. Children could explain how they made sounds louder and quieter and compare how louder sounds have stronger vibrations whilst quieter sounds have softer vibrations. Individuals could feel the strength of vibrations changing by lightly pressing finger tips to their throat whilst alternating between shouting and whispering.

Storm in a circle

Form a large circle and tell children that you are going to make a range of sounds with different parts of your body. The person immediately to your right should be the first person to copy your sound and, when they are doing this, then the person to their right and so on until everyone in the circle is eventually making the same sound. Explain that you will then make a new sound and they are to follow the same process a number of times.

Begin by making long, quiet 'sh' sounds, building louder to represent the wind and then rubbing the palms of the hands together softly before increasing pace and force. Next, clicking the fingers to represent light intermittent rain and then slowly patting hands onto thighs in a 'pitter patter' rhythm and building pace until it sounds like loud, heavy rain falling. Thunder can be represented by a single heavy jump and return to patting hands on thighs again. Gradually slow down to make tapping movements lighter and slower, returning to finger clicking with diminishing pace until complete silence falls upon the group again.

Ask children to discuss what they think the sounds represented. How did they know when the storm was at its peak or ending? How did they increase or decrease the volume of sounds? Children will be able to relate volume of sounds to the strength of vibrations depending on how hard or soft they were clicking their fingers or slapping their legs! There are some inspiring advertisements on television and the internet whereby groups of people have formed a 'choir of noise' to represent cars on a journey or extreme weather conditions and these can be commented upon in terms of how the volume of sound was increased or decreased depending on strengths of vibrations.

Working scientifically

- **Identifying differences, similarities or changes related to simple scientific ideas and processes**
- **Using straightforward scientific evidence to answer questions or to support their findings**

Make a clap-o-meter

Data loggers and sound meter apps are perfect for measuring the volume of sounds, as in the introductory activity for this topic. Groups of children could rehearse and perfect a piece of performance poetry, such as *The Sound Collector* by Roger McGough, and then perform this for the rest of the class. The strength of vibrations made by vigorous or lack lustre applause will show as a measurement of the volume of sound (in decibels) for children to record and compare for each group. In simple terms, the group with the highest volume of applause will win the task!

Working scientifically

- **Setting up simple practical enquiries, comparative and fair tests**
- **Making systematic and careful observations and, where appropriate, taking accurate measurements using standard units, using a range of equipment, including thermometers and data loggers**
- **Using results to draw simple conclusions, make predictions for new values, suggest improvements and raise further questions**

Statutory Requirement: recognise that sounds get fainter as the distance from the sound source increases.

A real-life situation, such as the positioning of the school fire bell or a baby monitor, will enable children to carry out a meaningful enquiry into what happens to sounds as the distance from the sound source increases. The investigation is best done outside, using a loud and constant sound source such as a ringing phone alarm, crying baby doll or sound effects app. Groups of children can measure the volume of sound using a data logger or sound meter when they are immediately next to the sound source and then continue to take sound readings as they move to an agreed distance, such as one metre at a time, away from the sound.

This activity is a great example of pattern seeking. Children could record results in a table showing distance from sound source and volume of sound and then plot a very simple line graph chalked out on the playground floor. To conclude, a comparative statement such as: 'The further away from the sound source, the quieter the sound' will be the icing on the cake for this topic!

Working scientifically

- **Asking relevant questions and using different types of scientific enquiries to answer them**
- **Setting up simple practical enquiries, comparative and fair tests**
- **Making systematic and careful observations and, where appropriate, taking accurate measurements using standard units, using a range of equipment, including thermometers and data loggers**
- **Recording findings using simple scientific language, drawings, labelled diagrams, keys, bar charts and tables**
- **Using results to draw simple conclusions, make predictions for new values, suggest improvements and raise further questions**

10
A Creative Approach to Teaching Forces and Magnets

Even the youngest of children will be amazed at how many pushes and pulls they encounter in just one day! As an unofficial introduction to forces, Year 2 children will explore 'Materials' to find out how they can change the shape of some solid objects using different types of pushes and pulls (squashing, bending, twisting and stretching) as described on pages 83-84. In Year 3, children will extend their learning to a simple understanding of friction and magnetic forces, and then again in Year 6 to a deeper appreciation of a range of forces including simple mechanisms.

Forces and Magnets in Year 3

It is possible to teach all of the statutory objectives for this topic under the scenario of a toy manufacturer contacting the children asking for their help with product ideas and improvement. The children then take on the role of toyologists (yes, this is a real type of scientist!) involved in designing, investigating and suggesting modifications during their correspondence with the company.

> **Statutory Requirement:** compare how things move on different surfaces.

Toyologist challenge (1)

Children receive a letter or email from a toy company who want to improve the performance of their popular 'Looping racer', which is a single looped track for toy cars to zoom along and whizz off the end. Feedback from eight-year-olds states that the cars are stopping when they reach the end of the track and children would prefer it if they kept travelling as far as possible along the floor. Scientists at the company think that adding a material to the end of the track might improve performance; they have sent a number of samples (these could include: aluminium foil, bubble wrap, tracing paper, fabric, newspaper, laminated paper, polythene bag, rough sandpaper etc pre-cut into 30 x 5 cm strips) for testing and would like the children to investigate and reply with any interesting findings.

Children should compare how toy cars move along the samples of materials by:

1 Guided rolling to feel how easy or difficult it is to move a toy car along each material
2 Pushing a toy car from one end of the material and observing how well or how far it moves

3 Making a simple ramp and comparing how fast or how far toy cars travel when rolled down a strip of each material attached to the slope – if done in this way, there are opportunities here for measuring using standard units and simple comparative and fair testing.

Encourage children to report their findings back to the toy company, recommending which surfaces might work well as an improvement to the track design and why they think this.

> Working scientifically
>
> - **Setting up simple practical enquiries, comparative and fair tests**
> - **Making systematic and careful observations and, where appropriate, taking accurate measurements using standard units, using a range of equipment**
> - **Reporting on findings from enquiries, including oral and written explanations, displays or presentations of results and conclusions**
> - **Using results to draw simple conclusions, make predictions for new values, suggest improvements and raise further questions**

> **Statutory Requirement:** compare and group together a variety of everyday materials on the basis of whether they are attracted to a magnet, and identify some magnetic materials.
> **Statutory Requirement: observe how magnets** (attract or repel each other and) **attract some materials and not others.**

Toyologist challenge (2)

The toy company would like to make a simpler version of the 'Looping racer' toy for younger children where they can guide a toy car along a flat track using a magnet. The scientists were thinking that all metals are attracted to a magnet but, in their tests, the metal cars were not!

They have had an idea that if they fix a magnetic material to the front of each car, the magnet will attract this and the car will move towards it. Children should investigate which materials would be most suitable for this using a wide range of objects such as: plastic spoon, wooden peg, different coins (please note:

some coins will be attracted to a magnet and some will not and this depends on the year in which they were made and what metals they have been made from), pebble, glass bead, rubber band, iron nail/nut / bolt/screw, steel and plastic coated paper clip, steel cutlery, brass key, aluminium foil, copper wire, fabric, card etc. They should record their results using simple scientific language including magnetic and non-magnetic.

Using simple sorting, grouping and classifying, children should be able to explain that magnetic materials are always metals but only a few metals are magnetic. They should identify that any metal with iron in it will be attracted to a magnet. Steel contains iron, so a steel paperclip, for example, will also be attracted to a magnet.

Children could fix some of the magnetic objects they have identified to the front of a toy car (with double sided tape or sticky tack) and use a magnet to move the car around the floor or table top. Some children might decide to draw a simple map on a mini whiteboard and move the car around the 'road'. Finally, they should inform the toy company what they have found out, explaining which materials are magnetic and would be best for the toy design.

Working scientifically

- **Setting up simple practical enquiries, comparative and fair tests**
- **Making systematic and careful observations**
- **Gathering, recording, classifying and presenting data in a variety of ways to help in answering questions**
- **Recording findings using simple scientific language, drawings, labelled diagrams, keys, bar charts and tables**
- **Reporting on findings from enquiries, including oral and written explanations, displays or presentations of results and conclusions**
- **Using results to draw simple conclusions, make predictions for new values, suggest improvements and raise further questions**

Statutory Requirement: notice that some forces need contact between two objects, but magnetic forces can act at a distance.

Toyologist challenge (3)

The toy company are delighted to have identified magnetic materials that could be fixed to the front of their car and then guided around a flat track using a magnet. The scientists are wondering if it would be possible to move the car without actual contact between the magnet and the magnetic material by holding the magnet a distance away from the car. Would the car still move towards the magnet? How far away from the magnetic material would the magnet need to be?

Children could use the magnetic materials identified in the previous challenge (such as coins, paper clips, keys, nails etc containing iron or steel) to investigate which can be moved with a magnet from the furthest distance away. They should come up with their own ideas for how they might do this, however, a simple way is to place a long ruler on a flat surface and then position the object at 0cm and the magnet at 30cm and then move the magnet closer to the object until it is pulled (attracted) towards it. They should measure and record the distance at which this happens.

Children should use their results to fix the 'most magnetic' object to the front of a toy car and use a magnet to move the car around the floor or table top at a distance. Can they explain how their car is able to move by magnetic force?

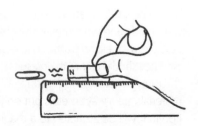

Working scientifically

- **Setting up simple practical enquiries, comparative and fair tests**
- **Making systematic and careful observations and, where appropriate, taking accurate measurements using standard units,**
- **Recording findings using simple scientific language, drawings, labelled diagrams, keys, bar charts and tables**
- **Reporting on findings from enquiries, including oral and written explanations, displays or presentations of results and conclusions**
- **Using results to draw simple conclusions, make predictions for new values, suggest improvements and raise further questions**

The floating paperclip

Although not explicitly linked with the toy scenario, children will always be fascinated by the 'floating paper clip' and it is a perfect way to show how magnetic forces can act at a distance. Children should cut a 30 cm length of cotton thread, tape one end down to the table top and fasten the other end to a metal paper clip. Hold the paper clip up against a magnet so that the thread is pulled taught in a vertical direction then, very slowly, lift the magnet a little higher and see if they can suspend the paper clip in air with nothing visibly supporting it. Ask children to predict what will happen if they hold a piece of paper in between the magnet and the paper clip as it is 'levitating' – will the paper block the magnetic force and the paper clip fall? What other materials can they try?

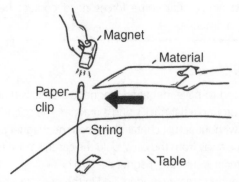

Working scientifically

- **Setting up simple practical enquiries, comparative and fair tests**
- **Making systematic and careful observations**
- **Using results to draw simple conclusions, make predictions for new values, suggest improvements and raise further questions**

Toyologist challenge (4)

The toy company is making great progress with the design of their new 'magna-car' and track. They would like to sell it in the science department of toy shops with an information leaflet all about magnets. They have sent a range of different sized and types of magnets and would like children to find out as much about them as they can.

Provide the class with a box or parcel 'sent from the lab' to include a range of bar magnets, horseshoe magnets, ring magnets, marble magnets and wand magnets of different shapes, sizes and strengths (if possible). Children should investigate and research using secondary sources of information to find answers to questions such as: Do you know the names of any different types of magnets? Which is the strongest part of a magnet? Can you name any parts of a magnet? How do you know which end is north and which is south? What else can you find out about magnets or magnetic materials?

Children could compile their findings into an appealing and informative leaflet to send back to the toy company. Gathering and presenting information is an important skill within the statutory requirements for working scientifically as well as writing with a purpose and for different audiences within the programme of study for English.

> Working scientifically
>
> - **Asking relevant questions and using different types of scientific enquiries to answer them**
> - **Recording findings using simple scientific language, drawings, labelled diagrams, keys, bar charts and tables**
> - **Reporting on findings from enquiries, including oral and written explanations, displays or presentations of results and conclusions**

Toyologist challenge (5)

The new 'magna-car' is almost ready for manufacturing but chief scientists would like to make one last modification. They have had an idea that one bar magnet could be fixed horizontally onto the roof of the car and another magnet could be used to act at a distance and pull the car around the printed track. They would like children to investigate whether a magnet can be used to attract another magnet and whether this works or not depending on which ends, or poles, of the magnets are facing each other.

Through open-ended exploration, children may be surprised to find that when a north and a north pole (or a south and a south) are placed together the magnets actually push, or repel, away whereas opposite poles facing result in magnets being attracted and pulled towards each other. Great fun can be had exploring this phenomenon!

Children should be encouraged to find patterns in results and form their own statements of conclusion, referring to how this will affect the direction travelled by the 'magna-car'. They could also secure a bar magnet onto the roof of a toy car (using sticky tack) and try this out for themselves.

Working scientifically

- **Setting up simple practical enquiries, comparative and fair tests**
- **Making systematic and careful observations**
- **Using results to draw simple conclusions, make predictions for new values, suggest improvements and raise further questions**

Forces in Year 5

> **Statutory Requirement:** explain that unsupported objects fall towards the Earth because of the force of gravity acting between the Earth and the falling object.

Gravity carousel

Children will learn a great deal about 'why unsupported objects fall towards the Earth' by exploring a range of intriguing practical activities and open thinking questions:

1 Individual children should put a 'splodge' of runny paint at the top of a piece of paper attached to an upright easel or taped to the wall. Ask: What do you notice about the direction in which the paint drips? What happens if you suddenly turn your paper a different way up? Why do you think this happens?

2 Secure the lid on a large pop bottle half-filled with coloured water and invite children to try tipping and tilting the bottle in different directions. Ask: What do you notice happens to the water level? Why do you think this happens?

3 Children could attempt a handstand or cartwheel. Ask: What happens to your hair (particularly long hair) when you are upside down? What happens when you stand back up again? Why does your hair do this?

4 Challenge children to jump up for as long as they can without holding onto anything. Ask: Can you stay in the air for more than 2 seconds? 5 seconds? Why do you think this?

5 Children could try throwing a ball up into the air for longer than 10 seconds. Ask: What happens to the ball? What is the longest time you can keep a ball up in the air for? Why?

Working scientifically

- **Reporting and presenting findings from enquiries, including conclusions, causal relationships and explanations of and degree of trust in results, in oral and written forms such as displays and other presentations**

- **Identifying scientific evidence that has been used to support or refute ideas or arguments**

> **Statutory Requirement:** identify the effects of air resistance, water resistance and friction, that act between moving surfaces.

It is a good idea to divide this statutory learning objective into at least three separate lessons or activities in order for children to investigate areas of friction, and then more specifically, air resistance and water resistance in greater depth.

Friction: Goalie gloves investigation

As an introduction to friction, there are some brilliant examples within the world of sports, such as how tennis racquets, cricket bats, football boots and goalie gloves are designed to provide maximum grip; why gymnasts put chalk on their hands; how skis, skates and toboggans are designed to slide quickly across snow and ice and how curling teams brush the ice frantically for increased glide.

Children may be surprised to learn that the use of goalie gloves only became common in the late 1960s and early 1970s, with many professional goalkeepers only wearing them prior to this to keep their hands warm! An investigation to compare a range of fabrics sent from a sports manufacturer provides a creative real-life context for children to find out which material provides the most friction and could be stitched to the fingers and palms of a new type of goalie glove.

Fabrics such as lycra (turbo stretch), sponge (foam grip), denim (dark demon), sandpaper (true grit) and bubble wrap (max-air) can be given fictitious names and tested in a range of ways to see which would result in the best grip when moved over a surface. For example, groups working together could use a force meter to measure the force required to pull a 1 kg weight across each sample of material.

Friction: Zip wire investigation

Groups of children could design and make a zip wire, including a harness, to carry a soft toy or Lego figure from one end of the classroom to the other, or even better outside from one tree to the next. Setting up a fair test investigation, whereby only the 'type of zip wire' (such as string, wool, plastic, wire, nylon) is changed and the time taken for descent is measured each trial, is a memorable way to investigate friction.

Working scientifically
- **Planning different types of scientific enquiries to answer questions, including recognising and controlling variables where necessary**
- **Taking measurements, using a range of scientific equipment, with increasing accuracy and precision, taking repeat readings when appropriate**
- **Recording data and results of increasing complexity using scientific diagrams and labels, classification keys, tables, scatter graphs, bar and line graphs**

- **Reporting and presenting findings from enquiries, including conclusions, causal relationships and explanations of and degree of trust in results, in oral and written forms such as displays and other presentations**

Investigating air resistance

The simplest way for children to experience air resistance for themselves is to run around outside and feel air pushing against them. They should also try this whilst holding a large sheet of card or an opened umbrella – can they feel a greater force of air pushing against them and slowing them down now? Children could make different sized parachutes from fabric or thick plastic (there are excellent links to them measuring and calculating the area of 2D shapes) and then investigating how long it takes for each one to fall through the air from an agreed height. Children should understand that a bigger parachute has a greater surface area for the air to push against and so will fall more slowly.

Dropping parachutes, paper spinners or even cake cases, blowing straw rockets or jumping on stomp rockets are all exciting ways for children to carry out fair test investigations. They should recognise when to change one variable, such as shape or size, and then observe or measure how this affects the time taken for the object to travel through the air.

As an alternative, children could investigate 'balloon rockets' travelling along a string or toy cars travelling across the floor both with different sized pieces of card attached to the front. Does the size of the card affect how far the balloon rocket or toy car will travel? Balloons would need to be inflated with the same amount of air and then released whereas toy cars could be pulled back with the same amount of force using an elastic band launcher in order to ensure a fair test. There are some great links to the maths curriculum through working scientifically when measuring the perimeter and area of shapes and distance travelled, as well as taking repeat readings and calculating average results.

Working scientifically

- **Planning different types of scientific enquiries to answer questions, including recognising and controlling variables where necessary**
- **Taking measurements, using a range of scientific equipment, with increasing accuracy and precision, taking repeat readings when appropriate**
- **Recording data and results of increasing complexity using scientific diagrams and labels, classification keys, tables, scatter graphs, bar and line graphs**
- **Using test results to make predictions to set up further comparative and fair tests**
- **Reporting and presenting findings from enquiries, including conclusions, causal relationships and explanations of and degree of trust in results, in oral and written forms such as displays and other presentations**

Investigating water resistance

The most obvious way for children to explore resistance in water is to take them to the swimming baths and let them feel for themselves how much more difficult it is to move against water compared to air, what it feels like to move through the water when travelling forwards compared to a side-wards direction and also to jump and dive in with different body shapes. Children will experience first-hand that the greater the surface area, the more resistance they encounter from the water.

Back in the classroom, groups of children could observe how different shapes of play-dough fall through water poured into a 2 litre pop bottle with the top cut off and then placed in a tray to catch any spills. Challenge them to make a shape with the most water resistance and then the least water resistance. Children could video record their most successful shapes and then play footage back using a slow motion app in order to make more accurate comparisons and measurements of time taken.

Working scientifically

- **Taking measurements, using a range of scientific equipment, with increasing accuracy and precision, taking repeat readings when appropriate**
- **Recording data and results of increasing complexity using scientific diagrams and labels, classification keys, tables, scatter graphs, bar and line graphs**
- **Using test results to make predictions to set up further comparative and fair tests**
- **Reporting and presenting findings from enquiries, including conclusions, causal relationships and explanations of and degree of trust in results, in oral and written forms such as displays and other presentations**
- **Identifying scientific evidence that has been used to support or refute ideas or arguments**

Statutory Requirement: recognise that some mechanisms, including levers, pulleys and gears, allow a smaller force to have a greater effect.

There are some innovative projects linked to the design and technology programme of study whereby children design and make models involving pulley, lever and gear systems. If you happen to have resources such as Lego and K'Nex in school, now is the time for children to explore and build! There are also creative links to the art curriculum whereby children could learn about the cartoonists, Heath Robinson (UK) and Rube Goldberg (USA), whose most popular drawings depicted complex mechanisms performing the simplest of tasks.

Investigating pulleys

Try not to overcomplicate activities – children do not need to build and investigate advanced pulley systems, although they could easily make a basic pulley using a skipping rope hung over a rolling pin, or a cotton reel with a thin wooden dowel pushed through the centre.

A simple, yet effective, activity is to tie a strong rope around the handle of a heavy object such as a large milk carton filled with sand and ask children to lift this to an agreed height. They should feel how difficult this is due to them working against the pull of gravity. Now throw the other end of the rope over a sturdy tree branch (or similar) and ask children to pull down on the rope to lift the container again. They should attempt to explain how the pulley makes the container feel easier to lift (although if they were to measure the force, it would be exactly the same) and this is because they are pulling down, with the force of gravity, rather than working against it.

Investigating levers

Set the scene that we need to lift a very heavy load to a certain height. We could use a lever and explain that the load goes at one end and we apply the effort (force) to the other end. For a lever to work, we need a fulcrum. Children can investigate where the best place is to position the fulcrum to ensure that the heavy load can be lifted most easily.

This investigation has some exciting cross curricular links with English, for example to the scene where Harry, Ron and Hermione meet Fluffy the three headed dog in *Harry Potter and the Philosopher's Stone*. Children could think about how to lift Fluffy while he is sleeping so that they can access the trap door below and retrieve the stone. There are also creative links to history topics such as how the ancient Egyptians and Greeks moved and lifted heavy materials in order to build pyramids and temples or how Vikings built dragon boats or long-ships.

A lever to investigate with could be a long wooden ruler (at least 30 cm) with a strip of masking tape to fix a fulcrum (pencil) in the centre of the numbered side. Small groups working together should fix a load, such as a 500 g weight, onto one end of the lever, labelled L for load, (sticky tack or double sided tape will keep it in place) and then push down on the other end, labelled E for effort, with a push-meter to make a measurement of the force required to lift the load in Newtons.

Children should investigate what happens to the force required to lift the load when the fulcrum is positioned at different measurements along the ruler.

Note: They might need different scaled push meters to measure this, for example: for a 400 g load, when the fulcrum is placed at 10 cm, the effort required is less than 5 N but when the fulcrum is placed at 40 cm the effort required is more than 20 N.

- **Planning different types of scientific enquiries to answer questions, including recognising and controlling variables where necessary**

- **Taking measurements, using a range of scientific equipment, with increasing accuracy and precision, taking repeat readings when appropriate**

- **Recording data and results of increasing complexity using scientific diagrams and labels, classification keys, tables, scatter graphs, bar and line graphs**

- **Reporting and presenting findings from enquiries, including conclusions, causal relationships and explanations of and degree of trust in results, in oral and written forms such as displays and other presentations**

11
A Creative Approach to Teaching Electricity

The 'Electricity' unit in Year 4 is now the first 'official' opportunity primary aged children have to learn about appliances and circuits in science. The topic is revisited and extended in Year 6, and teachers of both year groups should ensure plenty of opportunities for children to explore and investigate practically, using trial and error to advance their learning.

Electricity in Year 4

> **Statutory Requirement:** identify common appliances that run on electricity.

Mime it

Ask children to perform a mime which shows them using an electrical appliance, for the rest of the class to identify and name. A particularly revealing instance of this was when a Year 4 child mimed playing with a remote control car and when this was guessed correctly, another child protested, 'That doesn't run on electricity. That runs on batteries!' It is worth asking children to state whether the appliance they have identified runs on batteries or mains (or both) in order to show these methods are both acceptable examples of electricity.

Cut it out!

Giving small groups or pairs of children catalogues and magazines is a great way for them to identify common appliances that run on electricity by locating and cutting out as many examples in a given time such as ten minutes. They could use these images for a range of sorting and grouping activities, such as in which rooms of a house they might be found, and which appliances run on mains or batteries (or both). It is interesting to note how, when given a catalogue to browse, children tend to focus on games and toys that run on electricity rather than items for personal care or housework.

Working scientifically

- **talk about criteria for grouping, sorting and classifying (non-statutory notes and guidance)**

> **Statutory Requirement:** construct a simple series electrical circuit, identifying and naming its basic parts, including cells, wires, bulbs, switches and buzzers.

Sweet circuits

A fun and memorable way of introducing children to component names is to provide them with a selection of sweets including red laces, jelly worms and also liquorice allsorts. Ask children to choose a sweet that they think looks most like a cell/battery, for example the black liquorice roll, and then explain why they have chosen this. Continue for other basic components such as bulb, buzzer, motor and wires until children can name each component and justify their decisions. This activity can be extended by challenging children to build a 'sweet circuit' that would light a bulb or buzz a buzzer. Photographs can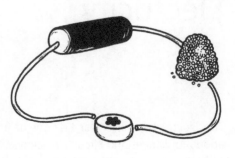

be taken and then labelled and compared with others in the class. This is a creative way to identify any misconceptions such as incomplete circuits or wires connected incorrectly and address these through children making equivalent circuits using real components.

> ### Working scientifically
> - **Recording findings using simple scientific language, drawings, labelled diagrams, keys, bar charts and tables**
> - **Identifying differences, similarities or changes related to simple scientific ideas and processes**

Working towards an electrical qualification

I have seen a number of excellent projects which approach the statutory requirements for this topic in terms of tasks or challenges that children must pass as part of their training to become a qualified electrician or electrical engineer. When the challenges are being introduced, individual children should record a self assessment of what they believe they are able to do. As each challenge is achieved, the teacher acts in an examiner type role by 'signing off' each skill and then presenting individual children with their completion certificate or official registration card when the relevant standard has been attained.

Challenge 1: Identifying and naming parts

A mixed up assortment of bulbs, cells and batteries, wires, motors, switches, buzzers, bulb holders and battery holders could be emptied out from an electrician's toolbox for children to explore. They could be given a contents or equipment list and asked to place an example of each item onto the list next to its corresponding name. Photographs could be taken as evidence of whether or not individual children have passed the first challenge on their checklist. A second attempt could be offered to those children who have made errors in identification.

Many children will not realise that a battery is made when cells are combined together. Encourage children to look at the voltage on the side of a range of cells and batteries in order to identify and name them correctly.

> ### Working scientifically
> - **Gathering, recording, classifying and presenting data in a variety of ways to help in answering questions**

Challenge 2: Building simple circuits

A list of simple circuits to make and tick off on the checklist should include:

- Can you make a circuit to light a bulb?
- Can you make a circuit to buzz a buzzer?
- Can you make a circuit to spin a motor?

Children who complete this quickly and easily could face extra challenges such as:

- Can you light a bulb in a circuit without using a bulb holder?
- What happens if you swap the wires over when connecting a buzzer in a circuit?
- What happens if you connect the wires to the same end (or terminal) of a cell or battery when lighting a bulb?
- Can you make a motor spin both clockwise and anticlockwise?
- What else can you find out about circuits?

Children could take photos or record short videos as evidence each time they successfully construct a circuit from the list. Alternatively, they could draw a pictorial representation of each circuit, labelling the components required, not necessarily using conventional circuit symbols at this stage; these will be introduced in Year 6.

> ### Working scientifically
> - **Using a range of equipment**
> - **Recording findings using simple scientific language, drawings, labelled diagrams, keys, bar charts and tables**

> **Statutory Requirement:** identify whether or not a lamp will light in a simple series circuit, based on whether or not the lamp is part of a complete loop with a battery.

Asking children to make a 'human circuit' is a great way of modelling the principles required for a basic understanding of how simple circuits work. One child could represent a 1.5 V cell and this could be signalled by them wearing a labelled sticker on their chest or a sign around their neck. Another child could represent a bulb (wearing similar identification labels) and the remaining children should stand in a circle, representing the wires, in order to join the 'human components' together.

Ask children to discuss what happens to the bulb when all the hands in the circuit are joined.

The child representing the bulb could put on a yellow cap to show how the bulb is lit when the circuit is complete. Ask two children to leave go of hands and question what will happen to the bulb now and why. The child representing the bulb could remove the yellow cap to show how the bulb is no longer lit when there is a gap in the circuit. Children should reinforce their learning by making and testing real circuits in the same way.

Challenge 3: Inspecting circuits

At this stage of their 'training course', children are called upon to identify the cause of a number of failed attempts at circuit making. Individual, pairs or groups of children should rectify the scenarios practically as well as produce a written or oral description of the problems encountered.

Examples of unsuccessful circuits to include could be:

- wire travelling from cell to bulb in one direction only
- wires connected to the same terminal of a cell
- a cell, buzzer and wires all connected correctly in an unbroken circuit (ensure that the wires are connected the wrong way round so the buzzer is not buzzing)
- a cell, motor and wires connected to a switch but the switch is open.

Working scientifically
- **Using a range of equipment**
- **Reporting on findings from enquiries, including oral and written explanations, displays or presentations of results and conclusions**

Statutory Requirement: recognise that a switch opens and closes a circuit, and associate this with whether or not a lamp lights in a simple series circuit.

Challenge 4a: Connect a switch

If your school is fortunate enough to have a good selection of electricity resources, it is worthwhile including a variety of switches such as: basic switch, push switch, slide switch, reed switch and toggle switch (any good educational suppliers will have these to order). Children will enjoy the challenge of exploring and investigating how real switches work in the circuits they have made during earlier challenges. Working out for themselves how to connect different types of switch to a simple circuit and then how to use the switch to control a buzzer, bulb or motor can be a very satisfying achievement for children of any age.

Challenge 4b: Design and make a switch

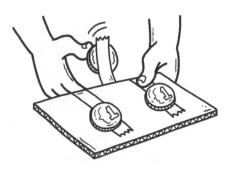

Children take the mantle of electrician or electrical engineer to design and make their own switch and then use this to control components in their own circuits. They might wish to use a range of resources such as card, paper clips, coins, aluminium foil, buttons, masking tape, sticky tape, split pins, glue and scissors. This activity should culminate in children sharing and demonstrating their switch designs with each other and, when it is time to move on and show someone new, the teacher should, of course, shout, 'Switch!'.

Note: This activity links perfectly to Challenge 5 whereby children distinguish between electrical conductors and insulators.

Working scientifically

- **Gathering, recording, classifying and presenting data in a variety of ways to help in answering questions**
- **Recording findings using simple scientific language, drawings, labelled diagrams, keys, bar charts and tables**

Statutory Requirement: recognise some common conductors and insulators, and associate metals with being good conductors.

There are some innovative products on the market to make circuits 'come alive' in the primary school and these can be used with excellent results to help children understand how circuits work and also which materials allow electricity to flow through them. Examples of such products include: 'cosmic balls', 'circuit sticks' and 'circuit maker breakers' and these can be found easily using a search online.

Children take delight in observing how one of the objects mentioned above, such as a 'circuit stick', might glow, flash or make sounds in a human circuit when everyone joins hands and then how this stops abruptly when the circuit is broken (two or more children let go of hands). Challenge children to suggest everyday items to connect a gap in the human circuit and predict whether this will enable the 'circuit stick' to light up or make sounds once more.

This is a superb activity for developing curiosity as well as sorting and grouping skills whereby children identify that, in addition to humans making excellent electrical conductors, only those objects made from metal complete the circuit successfully. Introduce new vocabulary by naming the metal objects as electrical conductors. The remaining items we will call non-conductors or insulators. This activity asks children to compare and group everyday materials on the basis of their properties, including electrical conductivity, which will be revisited in Year 5 (as described on page 91).

Working scientifically

- **Setting up simple practical enquiries, comparative and fair tests**
- **Making systematic and careful observations**
- **Using results to draw simple conclusions, make predictions for new values, suggest improvements and raise further questions**

Challenge 5: Conductor or insulator

Finally, to be considered as a qualified junior electrician, children must be able to identify conductors and insulators for themselves. As part of this challenge, they are invited to test a range of materials using a circuit they have built. Suggested materials to include could be: silver card, aluminium foil, pipe cleaner, shiny sweet wrapper, metal spoon, silver plastic spoon, silver coin, silver material, metal paper clip, plastic coated paper clip, tin can (baked beans etc.), aluminium drinks can and so on. Children should conclude that all metals conduct electricity, rather than any material that is silver or shiny.

Working scientifically

- **Setting up simple practical enquiries, comparative and fair tests**
- **Making systematic and careful observations**
- **Using results to draw simple conclusions, make predictions for new values, suggest improvements and raise further questions**

Electricity in Year 6

Children in Year 6 should feel confident in being able to construct simple series circuits, identify and name its basic parts as well as investigate electrical conductors and insulators. It is a good idea to begin this topic with a practical recap of work completed previously in Year 4 in order to address any misconceptions and also ensure that children are confident with the basic vocabulary involved.

> **Statutory Requirement: use recognised symbols when representing a simple circuit in a diagram.**

Who do you think you are?

Before any direct teaching of conventional circuit symbols, ask children to draw on a mini whiteboard what they think the symbols for a range of basic components (such as cell, wire, bulb, buzzer, motor and switch) are. You will be surprised at how accurate children's ideas can be at this very early stage. Keep their suggestions as evidence of prior knowledge as well as to document progress made later in the unit.

Match it up

Children could work in pairs to match up cards showing component names, component descriptions and circuit symbols. Once children have discussed their ideas and are confident that they have matched the cards correctly, they should collect the actual components from an assortment of equipment available to them. Completed sets should include: component name; component description; circuit symbol; real example of component. Class discussion could compare differences of opinion and then culminate in the correct matches being revealed, with lots of learning taking place.

Working scientifically

- **Recording data and results of increasing complexity using scientific diagrams and labels, classification keys, tables, scatter graphs, bar and line graphs**

> **Statutory Requirement:** associate the brightness of a lamp or the volume of a buzzer with the number and voltage of cells used in the circuit.

Learning about Alessandro Volta

Linking classroom activities with interesting stories of scientific discoveries throughout history is a great way to capture children's interest and enthusiasm. The story of Italian scientist Alessandro Volta, who invented the first kind of battery, will help children to understand and remember why we name the unit of electricity – the Volt. As in Year 4, encourage children to examine a range of different sized and shaped cells and batteries and locate the voltage for each one. Try to include a large 4.5 V battery and a small 9 V battery to show that it is not necessarily the biggest battery that has the greatest voltage.

Keeping it real

Children should use their own circuits to investigate what happens when two or more cells are used, as well as different voltage cells and batteries, to power a bulb or buzzer.

Note: Remember that the term battery is used to refer to a collection of cells.

A believable scenario such as the owner of a shop with dwindling customers aiming to make a brighter sign or a fire alarm in school that is not loud enough can be used to entice children to explore how these outcomes might be achieved. Children could take photographs of their successful (and unsuccessful) attempts and write a reply to the shop owner or school caretaker explaining what they have found out.

Working scientifically

- **Planning different types of scientific enquiries to answer questions, including recognising and controlling variables where necessary**
- **Using test results to make predictions to set up further comparative and fair tests**
- **Reporting and presenting findings from enquiries, including conclusions, causal relationships and explanations of and degree of trust in results, in oral and written forms such as displays and other presentations**

Statutory Requirement: compare and give reasons for variations in how components function, including the brightness of bulbs, the loudness of buzzers and the on/off position of switches.

Practical investigation in the 'Keeping it real' activity described prior to this could be extended through a fictitious email or phone call from the shop owner to thank children for their fantastic suggestions, however, the problem is that there is only one 1.5 V cell in the work box! Increasing the number or voltage of cells is no longer an option so what else could children suggest to make the shop sign brighter? In addition, the owners of next door's pet shop want to decrease the brightness of their sign and volume of door buzzer so that they do not frighten the animals!

Children might decide to investigate what happens when they add a switch into their circuit, increase or decrease the number of components in their circuit, make circuits bigger or smaller with more or less wires connecting everything together and also use thinner or thicker wires. Groups working together should have an opportunity to share what they have found out and a group email could be composed summarising the findings and advice from a range of enquiries.

Encourage children to record all of the circuits they have made by drawing diagrams on mini whiteboards or in note books using recognised symbols. Demonstrate how the wires in real-life might be curled and 'wiggly' but the wires in a circuit diagram must be drawn straight, meeting at right angles.

- **Planning different types of scientific enquiries to answer questions, including recognising and controlling variables where necessary**
- **Using test results to make predictions to set up further comparative and fair tests**
- **Reporting and presenting findings from enquiries, including conclusions, causal relationships and explanations of and degree of trust in results, in oral and written forms such as displays and other presentations**

Putting it into practice

Bring this topic to a climax with an exciting open-ended challenge in which children can revisit and consolidate the full programme of study for 'Electricity'. There are creative opportunities to link science with the design and technology curriculum, for example, individuals or small groups could design and make a simple burglar alarm system for a valuable item, a sensor to indicate when a bath contains the required amount of water, a 'light up' greetings card or an electrical game such as 'Buzz the wire' or 'Operation'. There should be opportunities for children to investigate through trial and error, evaluate and adapt their ideas until they reach a suitable solution to the problem.

Working scientifically

- **Planning different types of scientific enquiries to answer questions, including recognising and controlling variables where necessary**
- **Reporting and presenting findings from enquiries, including conclusions, causal relationships and explanations of and degree of trust in results, in oral and written forms such as displays and other presentations**

12
A Creative Approach to Teaching Earth and Space

The topic of 'Earth and Space' appears only once in the programmes of study for science (National Curriculum for England), however, children in Year 1 will learn about how day length varies as the seasons change (see page 59) and then in Year 3 as they find patterns in the way shadows change whilst learning about 'Light' (described on page 107). Year 5 children will develop their understanding of gravity during the 'Forces' topic (see page 123) and this is often linked to them learning about why astronauts float around in space or why we weigh more on Earth than on the moon.

There are creative links to be made with other curriculum areas, for example children could develop genres of writing such as poetry, science fiction, information texts and biographies as well as their learning in mathematics of shapes, relative sizes, distances and scale. The theme of space is an incredibly creative context for children to develop skills in art and music too, not forgetting opportunities to visit a local observatory or explore an inflatable planetarium for a day.

Earth and Space in Year 5

Statutory Requirement: describe the Sun, Earth and Moon as approximately spherical bodies.

It is likely that children in upper Key Stage 2 will have accurate ideas about the shape of the Earth, Sun and Moon. A quick way to assess this is to ask them to choose three different objects to represent the Earth, Sun and Moon from a wide range provided (such as all types of balls, PE hoops, pompoms, plastic counters, dice, packaging including cubes and cuboids, coins, cotton wool balls, play-dough and bottle tops). They could label each one with a sticky note and explain the reasons for their selections.

Ask children if anyone has chosen a cube shaped Sun or a pyramid Moon and to explain why. They could use secondary sources to examine real images taken from space to show the curved shape of the Earth, Sun and Moon. There are superb opportunities for them to plan a balanced argument or debate considering evidence for and against the common misconception that the Earth is flat.

When choosing their objects, children could also be encouraged to think about the relative sizes (although this is not a statutory requirement) and consider whether or not the Sun is bigger than the Earth and, if so, how much bigger and so on. They could research astronomical facts and statistics as evidence to support their final decisions.

- **Recording data and results of increasing complexity using scientific diagrams and labels, classification keys, tables, scatter graphs, bar and line graphs**
- **Identifying scientific evidence that has been used to support or refute ideas or arguments**
- **Recognise which secondary sources will be most useful to research their ideas and begin to separate opinion from fact (non-statutory notes and guidance)**

Statutory Requirement: use the idea of the Earth's rotation to explain day and night and the apparent movement of the sun across the sky.

Children could work in small groups, using simple equipment such as balls and torches to make their own models to show how and why we have day and night. This activity will provide a fascinating insight into children's pre existing ideas, including common misconceptions that the Earth orbits the Sun, that the Moon provides our light at night or the Sun moves around the Earth. Encourage children to use key vocabulary such as Earth, rotate, axis, Sun, lighter, darker, day and night in their explanations as they demonstrate and evaluate their models. They might also choose to stick a piece of sticky tack, Lego figure or a small flag onto their 'Earth' to represent themselves and where they live. Be sure to video record their final commentaries as evidence of their knowledge and conceptual understanding.

Children should understand that the Sun is the centre of our solar system and does not move whilst the Earth rotates in an anti-clockwise direction on its axis (an imaginary pole through the centre of the Earth). When the Earth rotates away from the Sun, it is becoming night and when the Earth rotates towards the Sun, it is becoming day. It takes the Earth 24 hours to complete one full rotation. A correct explanation of this will enable children to understand how, although it looks like the Sun moves across the sky during the day, it is actually the Earth that is rotating away from and towards the Sun.

To extend this activity, show children different times on a clock and ask them to rotate their model Earth to indicate where they would be relative to the Sun at this time.

Working scientifically

- **Recording data and results of increasing complexity using scientific diagrams and labels, classification keys, tables, scatter graphs, bar and line graphs**
- **Reporting and presenting findings from enquiries, including conclusions, causal relationships and explanations of and degree of trust in results, in oral and written forms such as displays and other presentations**
- **Identifying scientific evidence that has been used to support or refute ideas or arguments**

Statutory Requirement: describe the movement of the Earth, and other planets, relative to the Sun in the solar system.

Take the class outside and ask a child representing the Sun (they could wear a yellow cap and/or T-shirt to signify this) to stand still in the middle of the space as if they are the centre of our solar system.

Choose another child to represent the Earth (they could wear a label or sticker to signify this) and explain that, as well as rotating on its axis, the Earth also travels around, or orbits, the Sun. Ask 'the Earth' to walk at a slow and steady pace around the Sun in an anti clockwise direction. You could use a scaled model to determine the Earth's approximate distance from the Sun and draw a chalk circle on the floor at approximately one metre away from the Sun for the 'Earth' to follow in its orbital path.

Ask children to suggest how long it takes for the Earth to orbit the Sun and discuss how this takes 365 ¼ days, which is the equivalent of one year. This information could be added to Earth's label or sticker before discussing why we have a Leap Year every four years to account for the additional day added to our calendar.

Party on the planets!

Explain that the other planets in our solar system orbit the Sun in the same way as the Earth and invite individual children to represent different planets (again with labels or stickers). This is a good opportunity to assess whether or not children know the names of other planets as well as the order of their distance from the Sun (again, this is not a statutory objective but many children pride themselves on mastering this information).

The child representing the nearest planet, Mercury, should walk steadily in a circle at approximately 40 cm away from the Sun, being careful to remain in an orbital path (a chalk circle drawn on the floor may help with this). Children will observe how this takes less time than the Earth, as the distance to travel is much shorter. Explain that, if we were to live on Mercury, we could have a birthday party every 88 days! (Mercury could add this information to their label or sticker.)

Compare this to the distant planet Neptune and observe how long it takes a child to orbit the Sun (walking in a circle at almost 39 m away from the Sun). Explain that one year on Neptune takes 60,189 days (they should write this on their label or sticker) and, because this planet is much further away from the Sun, it would be a very long time in between birthday parties!

Children could estimate how often they might be able to host a birthday party if they lived on the remaining planets, thinking about distance away from the Sun and time taken to orbit. They could then research this information, using secondary sources, to find out how close or far away they were with their ideas.

Working scientifically

- **Recording data and results of increasing complexity using scientific diagrams and labels, classification keys, tables, scatter graphs, bar and line graphs**
- **Reporting and presenting findings from enquiries, including conclusions, causal relationships and explanations of and degree of trust in results, in oral and written forms such as displays and other presentations**
- **Identifying scientific evidence that has been used to support or refute ideas or arguments**
- **Recognise which secondary sources will be most useful to research their ideas and begin to separate opinion from fact (non-statutory notes and guidance)**

It could be you!

The current National Curriculum for science in England states that there are eight planets in our solar system: Mercury, Venus, Earth, Mars, Jupiter, Saturn, Uranus and Neptune and also that Pluto was reclassified as a 'dwarf planet' in 2006. In 2016, since publication of the curriculum, astronomers announced evidence for a ninth planet, 'Planet X', so far away beyond Neptune it is believed to orbit the Sun every 15,000 years! The new planet was spotted by a 15-year-old schoolboy from England, Tom Wagg, when searching through data during work experience at university. Tom had always been keen on science at school and is possibly the youngest person ever to have made such a discovery.

Children will enjoy carrying out additional research on this inspiring story and creating a newspaper article with an appropriate headline such as, 'School boy is over the Moon!' and to include interesting facts about planetary discoveries and fictional quotes from scientists as well as Tom's friends and family. There are creative links with the upper Key Stage 2 programme of study for English whereby children write for different audiences and purposes as well as use organisational and presentational devices to structure text and to guide the reader.

Working scientifically

- **Identifying scientific evidence that has been used to support or refute ideas or arguments**
- **Recognise which secondary sources will be most useful to research their ideas and begin to separate opinion from fact (non-statutory notes and guidance)**
- **Use relevant scientific language and illustrations to discuss, communicate and justify their scientific ideas and should talk about how scientific ideas have developed over time (non-statutory notes and guidance)**

Before children start learning about how the Moon appears to change shape, they should be secure in their understanding that the Moon is not a light source; it appears to 'shine' because it reflects light from the Sun. This can be modelled simply by showing them a foil wrapped ball in a dark area so they can observe that it does not shine. Now direct a lit torch to represent the Sun onto the ball and observe that it appears to shine because the light is reflecting off the foil surface.

Observing the phases of the Moon

At the very start of this topic, give each child a Moon diary or journal so that they can look outside every evening to observe and record the appearance of the Moon, paying particular attention to its shape. At the end of 28 days, children should return their diaries to school and discuss their observations, looking for patterns in data. Children could also use secondary sources such as an online 'phases of the Moon' calendar or calculator to find out the lunar phase for any given month. This could include significant dates such as when they were born or an important event in the future.

Working scientifically

- **Recording data and results of increasing complexity using scientific diagrams and labels, classification keys, tables, scatter graphs, bar and line graphs**
- **Reporting and presenting findings from enquiries, including conclusions, causal relationships and explanations of and degree of trust in results, in oral and written forms such as displays and other presentations**
- **Use relevant scientific language and illustrations to discuss, communicate and justify their scientific ideas and should talk about how scientific ideas have developed over time (non-statutory notes and guidance)**

Modelling the phases of the Moon

Children should understand that the shape, or phase, of the Moon depends on where it is in its orbit around the Earth. A simple model of this can be created in a dark classroom using a bright light source such as a projector or a table lamp with the shade removed to represent the Sun, a white polystyrene ball attached to a short stick or pencil to represent the Moon and a child to represent the Earth. They should face the light source (Sun), holding the Moon out at an arm's length and angled up higher than the top of their head. They should rotate slowly in an anti-clockwise direction (ensuring that the same side of the Moon always faces them) until they have completed one full 360° rotation on the spot. Spinning slowly on a revolving office chair works well too!

This model can be used to help children to understand that no matter where the Moon is in its orbit, half of it is always lit up by the Sun but this is not always what we see from Earth.

As they turn slowly, children should observe more and more of the Moon being lit, from new Moon to crescent to quarter to gibbous to full Moon (as they turn away from the light source) and then gradually less of the Moon being lit as they complete the Moon's orbit and a full lunar phase.

- **Reporting and presenting findings from enquiries, including conclusions, causal relationships and explanations of and degree of trust in results, in oral and written forms such as displays and other presentations**
- **Identifying scientific evidence that has been used to support or refute ideas or arguments**

What can we learn about the surface of the Moon? – a fair test investigation

Many teachers complain that there are few obvious opportunities to work practically when studying the topic of 'Earth and Space'. Children could recreate the surface of the Moon using trays half filled with sand and then investigate variables that might affect the dimensions of craters formed when meteorites hit. Examples of enquiry questions could include:

- How does the size of the meteorite affect the width of the crater? Children drop different sized spheres from the same height and then measure the diameter of indentations in the sand.
- How does the height the meteorite is dropped from affect the depth of the crater? Children drop identical marbles from different heights and then measure the depth of indentations in the sand.
- How does the shape of the meteorite affect the length of ejecta (surface of the Moon to be thrown out around the crater on impact)? Children sprinkle cocoa on top of the sand, drop different shaped objects from the same height and then measure the distance travelled by cocoa on impact.

Small groups of children working together should make their own decisions about how to control variables, take and record measurements and then relate their own conclusions to the formation of real craters on the Moon.

Working scientifically

- **Planning different types of scientific enquiries to answer questions, including recognising and controlling variables where necessary**
- **Taking measurements, using a range of scientific equipment, with increasing accuracy and precision, taking repeat readings when appropriate**

- **Recording data and results of increasing complexity using scientific diagrams and labels, classification keys, tables, scatter graphs, bar and line graphs**
- **Using test results to make predictions to set up further comparative and fair tests**
- **Reporting and presenting findings from enquiries, including conclusions, causal relationships and explanations of and degree of trust in results, in oral and written forms such as displays and other presentations**
- **Identifying scientific evidence that has been used to support or refute ideas or arguments**

Fiction versus fact

Look out for common scientific misconceptions found in young children's story books, such as the Moon is made of cheese and it changes shape because mice are nibbling at it or the Moon gives out its own light or it is possible for us to reach the Moon. Children could work as editors and identify 'incorrect science' in fiction books before drafting scientifically correct explanations or adding space related facts as footnotes. Some examples of books to use are: *The Loon on the Moon* by Chae Strathie and Emily Golden, *Goodnight Magic Moon* by Janet Bingham and Rosalind Beardshaw, and *Whatever Next* by Jill Murphy.

Working scientifically

- **Identifying scientific evidence that has been used to support or refute ideas or arguments**
- **Recognise which secondary sources will be most useful to research their ideas and begin to separate opinion from fact (non-statutory notes and guidance)**
- **Use relevant scientific language and illustrations to discuss, communicate and justify their scientific ideas and should talk about how scientific ideas have developed over time (non-statutory notes and guidance)**

Index

absorbency, in materials 82, 92
air resistance 130
animals including humans 17–42
Arcimboldo, Giuseppe 27
autumn
    investigating leaves colour change 60–61
    weather forecasting 61
    welly walks and scavenger hunts 60

binomial (two part) naming system 58
blood 38, 42
blood vessels 38
body parts 20–1
bones 31–32
    for protection 31
    for support 32

changing clocks
    in spring 65
    in winter 63
circuits 136
    building 137–8
    inspections 138
circulatory system 37, 39
    learning about 39

Darwin, Charles 69
data logging 110
digestive system 32–3
dissolving materials 93

Earth and space 145–7
    Moon (See Moon)
    party on planets 147–8
    research on 148–9
eating habits 19–20
electrical qualification, working towards 136
electricity
    circuits 136
    circuits building 137–8
    circuits inspections 138
    components 141

conductor 140
electrical qualification 136
insulator 140
locating and cutting out 135–6
miming 135
parts, identifying and naming 136–7
practice of 143
switches 138–40
Volta, Alessandro 141–2
evolution and inheritance
    animal adaptations 69–70
    fossil analogy 67–8
    fossil detectives 68–9
    plant adaptations 70–1
exercise and pulse rate 40–41

fats 29
five-a-day campaign 30
fizzy lemonade, making of 98
floating paperclip 126–7
flowering plants 6
food chain 35–6
food diary 26
forces and magnets
    air resistance 130
    floating paperclip 126–7
    friction 129–30
    gravity 128–9
    levers 132–3
    pulleys 131–2
    toyologist challenge 123–6, 127–8
    water resistance 130–1
fossil
    amber fossil 102
    analogy 67–8
    cast fossil 102
    detectives 68–9
    mould fossil 101
friction 129–30
    goalie gloves investigation 129
    zip wire investigation 129–30
fruits 7

germs 27
goalie gloves investigation 129
gravity 128–9
guessing games 76

healthy and unhealthy foods 26
healthy food habits 26
hearing 22
heart 37–8
Hirsch, Mark 59
human digestive system 32–3
hygiene 27

iDials 45
insulator, electrical 140
intestine, small and large 33
'I-spy' sheet 5, 45, 101

leaves, labelling of 7
leaves colour change 60–61
levers 132–3
life cycles 24
light
    data logging 110
    light maze 113–15
    shadow sculpture 110–11
    shadow size investigation 111–12
    sorting light sources 107–10
Linnaeus, Carl 56, 58
living things and their habitats 43–58
    animal classification 49
    articulate through art 45, 57
    classification using observable
        characteristics 55–6
    exploring opportunities 50
    human classification 48–9
    hunting and searching 44
    micro-organisms, classification of 56–7
    naming plants and animals 57–8
    observation over time 52
    physical sorting 51–2
    plant reproduction 53
    resources for identification of 45
    sorting and grouping 44
    trees 45

magnets 92
materials
    absorbency 82, 92
    collection of 77–8
    creating new materials 97–8

dissolving materials 93
feely boards, walls, books, handprints and
    collages 78–9
guessing games 76
investigation of 86
magnets 92
melting and freezing points 87–88
movements 83
properties and changes of 91–8
riddles and rhymes 81–2
ridiculous materials 81
see-through/not see-through (transparent/
    opaque) 79
separating solids and liquids 95–7
shock absorbency 82–3
solubility 94
solutions 94–5
stretch-ability 79–80, 92–3
testing of 82, 83–4
thermal conductivity 92
water cycle modelling 89–90
waterproof/not waterproof 79
melting and freezing points 87–88
micro-organisms, classification of 56–7
Moon
    fiction versus fact 151
    phases 149–50
    surface 150–1
mouth 19, 33, 34
movements 83
muscle 32

nutrition
    calculators 29
    labels, reading and comparing 29

oesophagus 33
O'Keeffe, Georgia 45
owl pellets, exploration of 36

physical properties, comparing and grouping by 100–1
physical sorting 51–2
physics
    See Earth and space
    electricity 135–43
    forces and magnets 123–33
    light 107–15
    sound 117–22
plants 5
    articulating through art 6, 8
    edible parts 9

flowering plants 6
fruits and vegetables 7
growing new plants from cuttings 54
leaves, labelling of 7
naming 57–8
necessary items for growth of 12
observing from bulbs 9–10
observing from seeds 10
parts of 8, 13
re-growing vegetables 53–4
reproduction of 53
roots 14
seeds 53
trees, identification of 7
water transportation 14–15
pollination 15
pulleys 131–2

rainfall 64–5
reverse thinking 118–19
rocks 99–103
appearance, comparing and grouping by 99–100
'I-spy' rocks 101
amber fossil 102
cast fossil 102
mould fossil 101
physical properties, comparing and grouping by 100–1
separating soil 103
roots 14

saturated fats 29
seasonal changes 59–66
autumn 60–1
spring 64–5
summer 65–6
winter 61–4
seeds 53
seeing, activities for 22
see-through/not see-through (transparent/opaque) 79
shadow
sculpture 110–11
size 111–12
shock absorbency 82–3
shopping bag sorting 85–6
smelling, activities for 22
smoking, impact of 41
snow 63–4
soap, and hygiene 27

soil, separating 103
solubility 94
solutions 94–5
sound 117–22
clap-o-meter 121–2
reverse thinking 118–19
storm in a circle 120–1
vibration stations 118, 119–120
spotter sheets 45
spring 64–5
changing clocks 65
rainfall 64–5
stomach 33
storm in a circle 120–1
sugar 30
summer 65–6
sunshine 66
temperature 66
sunshine 66
switches 138–40

teeth 34–35
brushing 28
temperature 63, 66
thermal conductivity 92
touching, activities for 22
trees 45
identification of 7

vegetables 7
vibration stations 118, 119–120
visits out and visitors in 17
Volta, Alessandro 141–2

water cycle modelling 89–90
waterproof/not waterproof 79
water resistance 130–1
weather forecasting 61
whole-class key 49–50
wind 62
winter 61–4
changing clocks 63
evergreen and deciduous trees 61–2
snow 63–4
temperature 63
wind 62

x-rays 21